-49963

BIR
Ref

The Art of
Walt Disney

from Mickey Mouse to the Magic Kingdoms

The Art of
Walt Disney

from Mickey Mouse to the Magic Kingdoms

Concise Edition

Christopher Finch

Virgin

Project Manager: Eric Himmel

Editor: Nicole Columbus

Designer: Judith Hudson

First published in Great Britain in 1999 by
Virgin Books
An imprint of
Virgin Publishing Ltd
Thames Wharf Studios
Rainville Road
London W6 9HT

A catalogue record for the book is available from
the British Library.

ISBN 0 7535 0344 1

Published in the USA by Harry N. Abrams,
Incorporated, New York

Printed and bound in China

Contents

Foreword by Roy E. Disney 7

Introduction 9

1 Early Enterprises 10

2 Mickey Mouse and Silly Symphonies 20

3 Hyperion Days 36

4 Five Animated Classics 48

5 Interruptions and Innovations 76

6 New Beginnings 90

7 A Second Flowering 100

8 Muskets and Mouseketeers 126

9 Beyond Film 138

10 Themes and Variations 146

Index 158

Foreword

I have a very clear memory of picking up Christopher Finch's wonderful book, *The Art of Walt Disney*, when it was first published in 1973, and thinking how long overdue it seemed. It was simply a beautiful book in every way: bright, articulate, and full of the whole panoply of emotions, from joy to terror to heartbreak to love, that are so integral a part of the Disney palette.

It seems clear that I was right about the book, because it has never been out of print since then, and it has even been updated during that span of years.

In 1973, Walt Disney had only been gone for a relatively few years, and the book might have seemed to be a kind of memorial. It is obviously much more than that, as its several revisions testify. It is a book about a living art, which has continued to grow and flourish through the years.

I'm sure I speak for all of us at the Disney Company, both now and in the future, when I say thanks, yet again, to Christopher Finch for this beautiful and timeless book.

Roy E. Disney

Introduction

The Walt Disney Company occupies a unique place in the history of American popular culture. No other major entertainment corporation is so marked by the imagination and persona of its founder. Walt Disney gave the world Mickey Mouse, single-handedly developed the animated feature film, and invented the modern theme park. More than thirty years after his death, his influence is felt more strongly than ever.

In 1972, I had the good fortune to be invited to write a book about the history of the Disney studio. *The Art of Walt Disney* was published the following year and has remained in print ever since. A 1995 edition gave me the opportunity to update the original text in order to reflect the achievements of the company since 1973, especially under the leadership of Michael Eisner, who became chief executive officer in 1984.

For this concise edition of the book, I have attempted to preserve its character and to retain all the essential information. The reader will find here not just the bare facts, but also anecdotal memories told in the words of men and women who were present at the birth of *Snow White* and who helped plan Disneyland® and EPCOT® Center. In addition, I have used this occasion to update the text once again so that *Toy Story* and new theme park attractions have their place alongside Donald Duck and the Silly Symphonies.

1 Early Enterprises

Walter Elias Disney was born into a modest Chicago household on December 5, 1901. His father, Elias Disney, Canadian by birth, was a small-time building contractor. In 1888, he married the former Flora Call, a schoolteacher from Ohio. At the time of Walt's birth, there were already three children in the family – Herbert, Raymond, and Roy. Walt was to develop a close relationship with Roy, who was nearest to him in age. A daughter, Ruth, was born later.

Times were hard in the building trade and in 1906 Elias pulled up stakes and moved his family to a forty-eight-acre farm outside Marceline, Missouri. Then as now, small farms did not offer an easy route to prosperity. Herbert and Raymond, in their teens, soon returned to Chicago. Walt and Roy stayed behind and were, of course, expected to help perform their share of backbreaking chores, but Walt found the time to develop a fondness for drawing. Before long, the farm was in financial trouble and in 1910 Elias sold the property and moved the family once again, this time to Kansas City, Missouri, where he bought a newspaper delivery business. Walt and Roy woke up at 3:30 every morning to meet the trucks of the *Kansas City Star* before beginning their rounds. Eight years older than Walt, Roy was soon in a position to escape this drudgery, but he stayed in close contact with his younger brother, offering good advice that included telling Walt he need no longer stand for the beatings Elias was in the habit of administering.

Walt's interest in drawing continued and he was allowed to enroll in Saturday morning classes at the Kansas City Art Institute. Along with a schoolfriend, Walt Pfeiffer, he also developed an interest in the theater, and "The Two Walts" made occasional amateur night appearances. Pfeiffer, who later became the Disney Studio manager, recalled that Elias disapproved strongly of anything theatrical so

Elias and Flora Disney in 1913

Walt Disney's birthplace at 1249 Tripp Avenue, Chicago, built by his father, Elias Disney.

"The Two Walts": Walt Pfeiffer, left, and Walt Disney pose in costumes they devised for one of their amateur night performances, c. 1915.

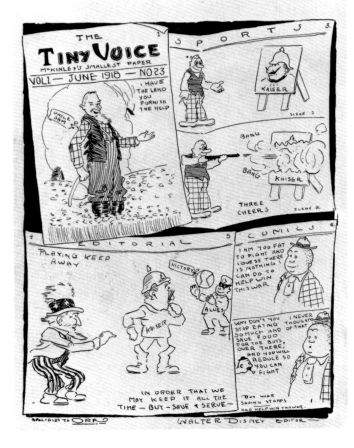

While at McKinley High School in Chicago, Disney contributed numerous drawings to the school paper, left, and, during his service in France, sent an illustrated letter to his former schoolmates, below

Walt would have to sneak out of the window when he had a performance. Walt was fascinated by the great silent movie comedians and would sometimes impersonate Charlie Chaplin on stage.

In 1917, Elias decided on yet another move, back to Chicago where he had purchased a part interest in a small factory. That summer, Walt worked as a news butcher on the Santa Fe Railroad, selling newspapers and candy. It was a job that helped shape his love of trains. Back in Chicago, he enrolled at McKinley High School, where he drew cartoons for the school paper. He also sought art training from a cartoonist named Leroy Gossett.

When America entered World War I, Roy joined the Navy, and Walt persuaded his mother to look the other way as he falsified his age so that he could join the Ambulance Corps. The armistice was signed before he reached France, but there was still work for ambulance drivers, and he established himself as his unit's unofficial artist, earning extra francs with such enterprises as camouflaging German helmets to make them look like snipers' helmets.

Walt Disney returned to the United States in 1919 and headed for Kansas City, where he found work in a local commercial art studio. There he made friends with another employee, Ubbe "Ub" Iwerks, a talented draftsman. They decided to go into business for themselves and achieved some modest success before Disney applied for a job with an organization called Kansas City Slide Company (a name that was soon changed to Kansas City Film Ad). This company made crude animated commercials for use in local movie theaters. Walt was hired and soon Iwerks followed him. The ambitious young pair had embarked on an adventure that would lead to both becoming Academy Award® winners.

Throughout the nineteenth century, scientists and inventors had intrigued the general public with a series of devices that could take a sequence of drawings and make them seem to move. All were rooted in the theory known as "the persistence of vision" first posited by the Anglo-Swiss doctor Peter Mark Roget, who also compiled the thesaurus. Most of these devices were variants upon a simple machine that had been conceived almost simultaneously by Dr. Joseph Antoine Plateau of the University of Ghent and Dr. Simon Ritter von Stampfer of Vienna. The Plateau-Stampfer device consisted of a drum mounted on a single shaft. The images to be viewed – they might portray an action such as a horse jumping a fence – were attached in chronological sequence as a strip along the inside rim of the drum. When this was rotated, an observer

The staff of Kansas City Film Ad Service, with Disney seated on the right-hand brick post. Ub Iwerks is standing seventh from the right

looking through a slit cut in one side of the drum would perceive an illusion of movement. This system developed into the zoetrope, which remained a popular toy for many years.

It was not until 1906 that the first animated film was attempted, when J. Stuart Blackton conceived a little entertainment called *Humorous Phases of Funny Faces.* The level of animation was rudimentary but it did demonstrate that it was possible to photograph drawings and make them appear to move, and this inspired other innovators. The greatest by far was Winsor McCay, who in 1908 put his comic strip character Little Nemo into an animated film. Later he toured the vaudeville circuit with a cartoon titled *Gertie the Dinosaur*, in which a very realistic dinosaur appeared to obey his commands. (He had chosen a dinosaur so that nobody could accuse him of tracing the image.)

Back to civilian life, Disney soon found work in a Kansas City commercial art studio

In 1913, two animated series were launched – *Colonel Heeza Liar,* devised by J. R. Bray, and *Old Doc Yak,* created by Sidney Smith. Soon a number of other animated characters were created, and an artist named Earl Hurd invented the idea of painting the animated figures on sheets of transparent celluloid. Previously, everything – including the static background – had to be drawn anew for each frame of the picture. Using Hurd's system, only the moving characters had to be drawn for each frame. A single background could be placed under the sequence of celluloid sheets – "cels" as they came to be called – and remain there until the scene was changed. This time-saving system would soon become standard throughout the industry.

As the technology improved, so did the ambitions of animators. In 1917, for example, Max Fleischer introduced the "Out of the Inkwell" series in which live action was combined with animation. The cartoons of the period were still crude, however. Plots consisted of slapstick gags strung together without structure, and broad exaggeration of physical features served as a substitute for character development.

This was the state of the art of animation when Walt Disney joined the staff of Kansas City Film Ad.

Walt behind the camera

The animation done at Kansas City Film Ad was, in fact, even cruder than anything coming out of the studios in New York, where the fledgling industry was then based. Kansas City Film Ad's animation consisted primarily of stop-action photography of jointed cardboard figures, a technique that precluded any serious effort toward naturalism. Nonetheless, it provided Disney (still just eighteen years old) with his basic training. Soon he borrowed a camera and tried some more ambitious animation on his own. The result was a little reel of topical gags, which he managed to sell to the Newman Theater, a local movie house. Over the next few months, a number of short commercials and illustrated jokes – known collectively as the Newman Laugh-O-grams – were made for the theater. Based on this initial success, Disney managed to raise enough capital to leave Kansas City Film Ad and set up on his own, retaining Laugh-O-grams as the company name.

He immediately set to work on a series of updated fairy tales, traditional in concept but incorporating modern artifacts such as automobiles and telephones. Six were made, and the four that survive provide evidence that at age twenty Walt Disney was already the equal of most other animation producers of the period. *Puss in Boots,* for example, is well animated and displays a nice sense of humor.

The title frame from a Laugh-O-grams cartoon, c. 1922

In the course of producing these cartoons, Disney began to build up an able staff that, in addition to Iwerks, soon included Rudolf Ising, Hugh and Walker Harman, Carmen "Max" Maxwell, and Red Lyon. Unfortunately, the Laugh-O-gram fairy tales did not sell, and the Disney production team had to scramble for alternative sources of income, even taking on a film devoted to dental hygiene. In 1923, Disney decided to try to save his venture by making a movie in which a human heroine would cavort with animated characters. The film that resulted was *Alice's Wonderland*.

For his Alice, Disney chose a little girl called Virginia Davis, who had some modeling experience with Kansas City Film Ad. The story begins as Alice discovers Disney seated at his drawing board with a sketch he has drawn of a dog kennel. An animated dog appears from the kennel, and before she knows what is happening, Alice finds herself involved with a whole menagerie of animals, including a quartet of lions who chase her over a cliff. The surviving print, however, is incomplete.

Alice was combined with hand-drawn animals by photographing Virginia Davis against a white background and then combining this footage, in the printing process, with another strip of film on which the animation had been recorded. The technique worked well, but before the movie was sold Disney's credit was exhausted, and he was forced to close the Kansas City studio. The time had come to pursue his career elsewhere. New York was the logical place for an animator to go in those days, but Walt Disney chose Los Angeles,

Disney at work in the Laugh-O-grams office, 1922

in part because his brother Roy was there in a veterans' hospital, recuperating from a bout with tuberculosis. In the summer of 1923, Walt Disney, age twenty-one, took a train west, carrying *Alice's Wonderland* with him as a sample.

Almost as soon as he arrived in Hollywood, Walt built an animation stand in a garage belonging to his uncle. On October 16, 1923, he signed a contract with New York–based distributor Margaret J. Winkler for a proposed series of Alice comedies, the first of which would be produced out of a space behind a real estate office that Walt and Roy had rented. The initial contract called for one movie a month, and Disney was able to persuade Virginia Davis's parents to bring her out to California to continue playing the lead.

Margie Gay poses with, left to right, Ham Hamilton, Roy Disney, Hugh Harman, Walt Disney, Rudy Ising, Ub Iwerks, and Walker Harman

After a shaky start, the Alice series became a modest success. Virginia Davis was replaced, briefly, by Dawn O'Day, and then by Margie Gay, who held the role for most of the series.

Additions to the animation staff were necessary, and Disney brought out several of his Kansas City associates, most notably Ub Iwerks. A new employee was an Idaho girl named Lillian Bounds. Often she worked late, and Walt would give her a ride home. A romance blossomed, and in July 1925, the pair was married. Walt's brother Roy had already married his Kansas City sweetheart, Edna Francis.

The studio was expanding and on July 6, 1925, four hundred dollars was deposited to secure a lot at 2719 Hyperion Avenue, near Griffith Park. A single-story building was erected, and this formed the nucleus of the plant that was to serve as the company's base for the next fifteen years.

By 1927 it became evident that Disney would have to find a replacement for the Alice comedies, which, after sixty episodes, had run their course. Work began on a new, entirely animated series that would feature an Iwerks-designed character named Oswald the Lucky Rabbit.

Oswald was a likable little character, all soft curves and energy. With him, Disney equaled – and perhaps surpassed – the best products of his competititors. This was reflected in the series' box-office success. There was just one snag. Margaret Winkler had married a man named Charles Mintz, who had a deal with Universal Pictures, and Disney had signed a one-year deal with Mintz. At year's end, Walt

Margie Gay as Alice with animated friends and director Walt Disney

The original Alice was Virginia Davis, whom Disney brought out from Kansas City to star in the series

Early Alice Comedies involved a good deal of live-action filming. Clowning on the Alice set: Rudy Ising holding the hose; under the umbrella are Hugh Harman, Ub Iwerks, and Walt Disney

and Lillian Disney embarked for New York expecting to renegotiate Disney's contract with Mintz, with provisions for a modest increase in income. Instead of offering an improved contract, Mintz actually proposed one that would entail a *reduction* of income for the studio. Obviously Disney could not accept such a deal, which was what Mintz was counting on. He had decided to repossess Oswald. The rabbit's name belonged to Mintz, not Disney, and several top Disney animators had agreed to take over the series, working for less money.

Disney was shocked and crushed. It is not difficult to imagine the thoughts that must have gone through his head as he and Lillian returned to California. His team was depleted but it still included his two most important early associates, his brother Roy and Ub Iwerks, who was given a partnership in the company. More important, Walt Disney had faith in his own abilities. He had reached the age of twenty-six after touching many of the bases of hardship that had come to seem paradigmatic of America in the first quarter of this century. His personal creed must have included the belief that success does not come easily.

Standing in front of their storefront studio, Walt and Roy Disney with, left to right, Walt's wife Lillian, his sister Ruth Disney, and Roy's wife Edna

The page of story continuity sketches for an Oswald cartoon, right, illustrates how cartoon stories were worked out in this period. Drawings from a model sheet, below, show that Oswald anticipated some of the physical characteristics of Mickey Mouse

2 Mickey Mouse and Silly Symphonies

It seems appropriate that the birth of Mickey Mouse – a creature of mythic stature – should be shrouded in legend. Walt Disney is said to have conceived Mickey on the train, returning to Hollywood after his angry encounter with Mintz. There is no reason to suppose that this is not essentially true, but over the years the story became so polished by repetition that it began to lose its sense of reality and take on the character of folklore. A further dimension was added to the legend by the fact that Disney had supposedly managed to tame a mouse in his old Kansas City studio, a mouse he called Mortimer. That name is reported to have been his first choice for his new character, but it was soon switched to Mickey, supposedly because Lillian Disney thought Mortimer too pompous for a cartoon animal.

What we can be reasonably sure of is that the Mickey Mouse who made his debut in New York City in 1928 resulted from a collaborative effort between Walt Disney and Ub Iwerks. Easily the best animator of the day,

Iwerks was largely responsible for defining Mickey's physical characteristics, although doubtless Disney had considerable input into the process. Mickey bore a family resemblance to Oswald, but the figure was made more compact. He was constructed from two large circles, one for the trunk and one for the head, to which were appended two smaller circles, representing ears, along with rubber-hose arms and legs that terminated in plump hands (ungloved at this early stage) and large, booted feet that provided him with stability. He was also equipped with a long, skinny tail, a plum-shaped nose, and button eyes. He was designed for maximum ease of animation (circular forms are easier to animate effectively), but beyond that Mickey was provided with something that was new to the medium: a real personality.

The gift of personality was Walt Disney's most lasting contribution to Mickey's success. Iwerks's draftsmanship made the whole thing work, but it was Disney's control of the situations in which the mouse was featured that

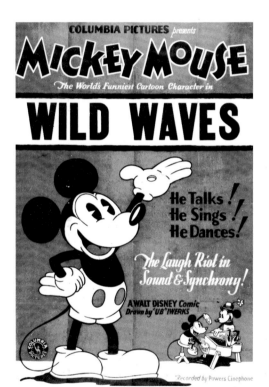

Mickey Mouse was originally drawn
by Ub Iwerks, top, who was given
credit in early publicity; bottom: an
early poster.

permitted the character's personality to develop.
He had grasped the notion that cartoon characters should seem to think, and he devised an
approach to storytelling that made this possible.

Another factor that made Mickey an
immediate hit was that he had the good fortune to be the right mouse at the right place
at the right time. Disney had begun work on
two Mickey cartoons – *Plane Crazy* and *The
Gallopin' Gaucho* – when the movie industry
was thrown into chaos by the runaway success
of *The Jazz Singer,* the first talking picture to
catch the imagination of the public. Walt
Disney was quick to see that his future would
depend upon wedding sound to the cartoon
medium. To do this properly, he realized,
would demand care and imagination. Putting
the two existing projects aside, he began planning a new Mickey cartoon specifically for
sound – a movie in which the on-screen actions
of his animated creatures would be carefully
synchronized with a strongly rhythmic sound
track, which featured both music and precisely
timed sound effects.

No one at the studio had any solid knowledge of musical theory, but a young animator
named Wilfred Jackson played the harmonica
and, because his mother was a music teacher,
was familiar with the metronome. This, he
suggested, might provide a way of matching
a musical beat to the sequence of film frames.

Les Clark, also a young animator at the
time, has described how the system worked:

"We could break down the sound effects so
that every eight frames we'd have an accent . . .
or every twelve frames. And on that twelfth
drawing, say, we'd accent whatever was happening – a hit on the head or a footstep or whatever it would be, to synchronize to the sound
effect or the music."

-Main Title-

Orchestra starts playing opening
verse of ' Steamboat Bill ',
as soon as title flashes on.

The orchestration can be so
arrainged that, many variations
may be included before the title
fades out.

It would be best if the music
was arrainged so that the end of
a verse would end at the end of
the title...... and a new verse
start at beginning of the first
scene.

Scene # 1.
Opening effect of black foliage
passing by in front of camera
gradually getting thinner until
full scene is revealed

Action......Old side'wheel river
steamboat paddleing down stream.
The two smoke stacks work up
and down alternately.... shooting
black chunks of smoke out as they
shoot up....smoke makes stacks
bulge out as it goes up and out.
(16 drawing cycle) 12 Ft. from
opening, the Three whistles on top
of cabin squat down before they
whistle tune ' TA--DA-DE-DA-DA---
DA-DA-'....2 Ft. of action after
whistle and out.

Scene # 2.
Close up of Mickey in cabin of
wheel'house, keeping time to last
two measures of verse of ' steamboat Bill '. With gesture he starts
whistleing the chorus in perfect
time to music....his body keeping
time with every other beat while
his shoulders and foot keep time
with each beat. At the end of every
two measures he twirls wheel which
makes a ratchet sound as it spins.
He takes in breath at proper time
according to music. When he finishes
last measure he reaches up and pulls
on whistle cord above his head.
(Use FIFE to imitate his whistle)

The first page of the *Steamboat Willie* continuity script. Disney kept this souvenir of his first major breakthrough in his office

By setting the metronome to correspond to the regular animated accents, a rough sound accompaniment could be improvised. One legendary evening, Disney and his handful of coworkers presented to an audience of wives and girlfriends a short sequence from the new Mickey Mouse film that would be titled *Steamboat Willie*. Roy Disney projected the film, while his brother – along with Iwerks, Jackson, Clark, and a few others – improvised their sound accompaniment live in another room, all of them working carefully to the beat of the metronome. Jackson played his harmonica, and the others provided sound effects with cowbells, slide whistles, tin pans, and the like.

This crude experiment convinced Walt that he was on the right track, and by September of 1928, a score had been committed to paper with the help of a professional arranger. Disney set out for New York, where he could find unlicensed sound equipment, and hired Carl Edouarde, a well-known Broadway musician, to conduct a recording session. It was a disaster. The Disney team had developed a crude system – probably using flashes blazed onto the print of *Steamboat Willie* that was projected during the session – for indicating the tempo at which the orchestra should play. Apparently Edouarde did not feel inclined to be dictated by so coarse a device. Disney was forced to cable California for more money and try again. He had the film reprinted with the addition of a bouncing ball system used to indicate the beat and tempo. This time everything went perfectly. *Steamboat Willie* had its soundtrack and Mickey Mouse was ready to make his debut.

This occurred at Manhattan's Colony Theater, where audiences were so enchanted by the cheeky rodent's antics that the movie was picked up by the prestigious Roxy Theater. The film was greeted with even greater enthusiasm there, and Disney was offered a distribution deal by an entrepreneur named Pat Powers. Walt would have preferred to sign with one of the big studios, but this was not

In *Steamboat Willie*, 1928, the first cartoon to feature a fully synchronized sound track, Mickey and Minnie transform the cargo of a riverboat – including livestock – into an orchestra

forthcoming; he therefore agreed to a one-year pact with Powers and hurried back to Hollywood to add sound to *Plane Crazy* and *The Gallopin' Gaucho*, while work began on two more Mickey cartoons.

The Mickey Mouse who hit the movie screens in the late twenties was not quite the well-behaved character we are familiar with today. He was mischievous and even displayed a streak of cruelty (which soon disappeared), but from the outset he had that germ of real personality that set him apart from his predecessors. Minnie was with Mickey from the very first and, in *Steamboat Willie,* the pair of them cavort with a cargo of livestock, using the various animals as musical instruments on which to improvise "Turkey in the Straw."

Mickey needed a voice, of course, and this was provided by Walt Disney himself, who would continue to speak for the Mouse (as he was called at the studio) for two decades.

The early Mickey shorts established Mickey and Minnie as creatures invested with special powers – they were no ordinary mice. They acted out roles that parodied the foibles of men and women. In this respect, they belong to a tradition that goes back to Aesop and Aristophanes, and audiences were fascinated to see that tradition reborn on the screen, especially with the addition of sound effects and music.

When *Steamboat Willie* was released, Walt Disney was twenty-six years old. His operation was tiny by the standards of the big studios, but he had his foot on the first rung of the Hollywood ladder – perhaps even the second.

A number of new Mickey cartoons appeared in 1929. Within the space of a few months, the Mouse acquired gloves, shoes, and a more endearing manner. An important technical advance was the decision to record the

The Gallopin' Gaucho, **top, was the second Mickey Mouse cartoon to be made, but it was produced as a silent film and not released until a sound track had been added.** *The Karnival Kid,* **1929, bottom, used gags derived directly from earlier situations devised for Oswald**

An early Mickey Mouse model sheet which shows the basic simplicity of his design

In *Blue Rhythm*, 1931, Mickey appeared as an entertainer.

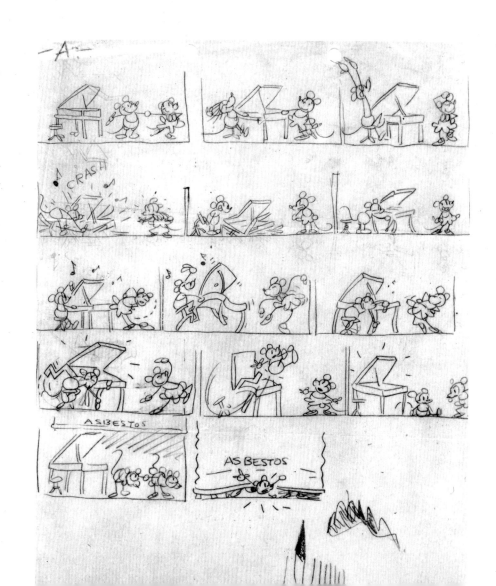

Rough story ideas for Mickey Mouse shorts were often worked out in thumbnail sketches, as in this example by Wilfred Jackson

Walt Disney at his desk, c. 1931, top.
In 1930, Carl Stalling, seen at the
piano, bottom, composed "Minnie's
Yoo Hoo" as a theme song for Mickey.
Seated alongside Stalling are Jack
King and Ben Sharpsteen, two of the
animators Disney had imported from
New York. Standing, left to right, are
Johnny Cannon, Walt Disney, Bert
Gillett, Ub Iwerks, Wilfred Jackson,
and Les Clark

sound track of any given film before animation
began. That way, the animators could work to
the rhythmic accents established in the score.
To handle the musical side of the business,
Disney brought in Carl Stalling, an old Kansas
City acquaintance who had years of experience
accompanying silent movies, a background
that served him well in his new career.

Stalling was a hard-nosed individual who,
unlike most of the younger Disney employees,
was not afraid to clash with his boss. Frequent
arguments occurred over the relative importance of music and visuals in an animated
cartoon. Differences were eventually settled
in an interesting way: the studio would produce two series. In the Mickey pictures, action
and gags would come first, and the music
would serve to underline them. In another
series, music and animation would be blended
to provide a totally new kind of experience.
This series was called the "Silly Symphonies."
The first of these to appear, in 1929, was *The
Skeleton Dance*, in which skeletons prance in a
cemetery to macabre music Stalling based on
Edvard Grieg's "March of the Dwarfs."

Although not as popular as the Mickey
Mouse cartoons, the Symphonies did well.
Early examples dealt with subjects as varied
as nightlife in a toy store and a china plate on
which the design comes to life. At first they
had little real focus, but it should be emphasized how original they were and how important in paving the way for things to come.

In 1930, another personnel crisis hit the studio
as Ub Iwerks and Carl Stalling quit the Disney
operation. Iwerks's departure occurred when
Disney's contract with Pat Powers came due
for renewal. Like Charles Mintz before him,
Powers underestimated Disney's importance
to the company's success. Powers thought that
Iwerks was at least his equal in talent, and,
behind Disney's back, he offered the animator
a series of his own. When Iwerks accepted,
Powers promptly went to the Disneys and
offered to tear up his contract with Iwerks if

Typical gags from 1931 Mickey Mouse short *Mickey Cuts Up*

they would agree to his terms. Walt and Roy refused, and Iwerks, caught in the middle, left to make cartoons for Powers.

Stalling left at about the same time, apparently because he was convinced that without Iwerks the Disney bubble would burst. (Later, he would resurface as the musical director for Warner Brothers' Looney Tunes and Merry Melodies.)

Unperturbed, the Disneys signed a new distribution contract with Columbia Pictures, and the escalating popularity of Mickey Mouse ensured the studio's continued success. By the end of 1930, Mickey had become an international celebrity. Known in Italy as Topolino and as Miki Kuchi in Japan, the Mouse continued his adventures, saving Minnie from danger, confronting the villainous Pegleg Pete in various exotic locales, and performing to audiences of enthusiastic animals whose taste in music ranged from ragtime to violin concertos. A simple-minded bloodhound made an appearance in a 1930 picture called *The Chain Gang* and developed before long into Mickey's faithful companion, Pluto. Other characters, such as Horace Horsecollar and Clarabelle Cow, briefly became costars, but their personalities offered relatively little for the animators to work with and their roles soon shrank.

By 1931, Mickey was important enough for *Time* magazine to devote a feature article to him. The production staff by then numbered more than forty and included a full-fledged story department that provided the forum in which Walt Disney could shape the films that bore his name. Stories were planned visually as much as verbally. At first they were worked out comic-strip fashion in notebooks. Soon, though, the studio pioneered the storyboard, the idea for which is generally attributed to a Disney artist named Webb Smith. Smith conceived of the notion of making each of his drawings on a separate sheet of paper and pinning them in sequence to a bulletin board. The story for an entire short could be accommodated on a single large board, and thus the director, or anyone else involved with the production, could see the elements of an entire movie spread out in front of him. If changes had to be made, drawings could be moved or taken down and replaced. It was the ideal method for developing an animated film, and it was perfectly suited to Disney's style. He no longer drew, but he could shape the movie at

In 1929, Disney launched a new series of cartoons which he called Silly Symphonies. The first was *The Skeleton Dance*, which featured some imaginative animation by Ub Iwerks set to a macabre score devised by Carl Stalling

27

From the very first, the Silly Symphonies touched a wide variety of subjects and moods. Illustrated here are *Winter*, top, and *Pioneer Days*, bottom, both 1930

the storyboard phase, controlling the overall structure and pushing his story artists to new heights of invention.

By the end of 1931, Disney's demand for constant improvement had driven the cost of a single eight-minute cartoon to more than $13,000 – a phenomenal amount for the period. (Other studios might spend $2,500 on a comparable picture.) Despite its success with the public, the studio was barely breaking even, and in 1932, another innovation drove costs still higher. In that year, Disney released a Silly Symphony called *Flowers and Trees*, which caused a sensation in the industry because it was in full color.

By today's standards, *Flowers and Trees* is a strange mixture of charm and absurdity. At the time, however, color made it a valuable property, and Disney signed a deal with Technicolor to have exclusive animation rights to the use of their new three-strip system for the next two years. (The system was so named because it required three strips of film to produce a full chromatic range.) For the time being, the Mickey cartoons continued to be made in black and white, but the Symphonies took full advantage of the potential of color. Almost at once they became more inventive. *Flowers*

and Trees was followed by *King Neptune* and *Babes in the Woods*, both of which display tighter structure and livelier action than anything previously seen in the series.

One thing that contributed to their inventiveness was the 1932 addition to the staff of the Swiss-born artist Albert Hurter. Hurter was steeped in the traditions of European folklore and gothic fairy tales. From the moment of his arrival at the studio, Disney realized that Hurter had a special talent and assigned him to produce what became known as "inspiration drawings" or "concept art." This is to say that he spent his time developing visual ideas for future projects and improvising on themes that might trigger the imaginations of story men or animators. As the studio continued to develop toward more ambitious projects, Hurter's presence was felt more and more strongly, and in 1933 he designed the settings and main characters for what turned out to be Disney's greatest hit up to that time, the famous *Three Little Pigs*.

It is hardly necessary to recapitulate either the plot of this Silly Symphony or the success of Frank Churchill's hit tune "Who's Afraid of the Big Bad Wolf?" The movie was a smash. Theaters retained it week after week and it came to be seen as an archetypal parable about

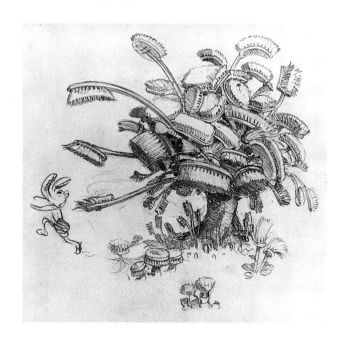

In addition to his contributions to specific movies, Albert Hurter spent much of his time producing casual drawings like this one, which would be circulated among directors, story men, and animators on the chance that they might spark an idea for a gag or even for an entire cartoon

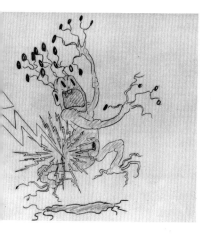

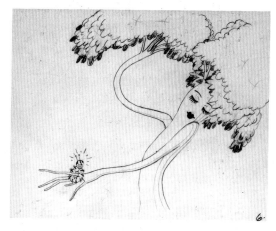

Flowers and Trees, 1932, has a
special place in the history of animation as the first cartoon to be made
in full color. From this point on,
all Silly Symphonies were produced
in the Technicolor® process

the Great Depression (an interpretation Disney dismissed as nonsense, saying the movie was intended as entertainment and nothing more). The following year, 1934, saw the production of several excellent Symphonies, including *The Tortoise and the Hare*, *Grasshopper and the Ants*, and *The Wise Little Hen*, each a moral fable and all showing how proficient the studio had become at structuring mini-dramas and at establishing character with a few strokes of the animator's pencil.

    The Wise Little Hen introduced a new voice talent and a new character, who, within a year, was ready to challenge Mickey as Disney's star attraction. This character was Donald Duck, and the man who provided him with a voice was Clarence "Ducky" Nash. Until Disney discovered him, Nash had worked for

In 1933, Walt Disney produced *Three Little Pigs* - a cartoon which had an extraordinary impact on the American public. Its hit tune, "Who's Afraid of the Big Bad Wolf?" swept the nation. Many people saw this film as Disney's comment in fable form on the Depression era. Whatever his motives for making it, it did display a marked advance in terms of story-telling and character development

a dairy company, entertaining children with animal imitations. One of these evolved into Donald's ill-tempered quack.

In his first screen outing, Donald had a relatively modest role as a dyspeptic creature who feigned a bellyache every time the Wise Little Hen asked for assistance. At that time, too, he sported a rather pointy beak that was modified to its present dimensions as the Duck went on to costar with Mickey in cartoons such as *Orphan's Benefit* (1934). So meteoric was his rise that by his first birthday the *New York Times* devoted an editorial to him, suggesting he might soon eclipse Mickey.

Meanwhile, other characters such as Pluto and Goofy began to reach for stardom. Pluto owed much of his success to animator Norm Ferguson, who, for the 1934 cartoon *Playful Pluto,* took a gag involving the pup's

entanglement with a ribbon of sticky flypaper and turned it into a classic of comic animation. Similarly, animator Art Babbitt took a minor character named Dippy Dawg and devised some business with a piano that transformed him into Goofy, the personification of cheerful incompetence. (Goofy's unforgettable, self-deprecating chuckle was provided by story artist Pinto Colvig.)

Mickey, meanwhile, had become a national symbol, and as such he was expected to behave properly at all times. If he occasionally stepped out of line, the studio would be inundated with letters from angry parents and watchdog organizations wary of the Mouse's influence on the children of America. It was becoming harder and harder to find comic situations for him that would not give offense in some quarter. Eventually he would be pressured into the

Lullaby Land, 1933, left, presents a child's dream adventures in a land-scape metamorphosed from the patchwork quilt that covers his bed. The following year, in *The Goddess of Spring*, below, Disney artists attempted to revive the myth of Pluto and Persephone

A layout drawing for *The Wise Little Hen*, 1934, illustrates the scene in which Donald Duck made his debut. He is discovered dancing a hornpipe on the deck of a somewhat decrepit barge

A general view of the Hyperion Avenue studio, c. 1933

role of straight man, but the gradual change had not yet eroded the core of his personality, and the Mickey cartoons of the mid-thirties were consistently inventive.

By this time, Disney artists had learned how to convey a shift in mood by a subtle change in expression, or by an almost imperceptible alteration of physical attitude. As the Disney team perfected its skills, it continued to expand, drawing to itself talented young men attracted to Hyperion Avenue by its spectacular advances. The fact that the Depression was at its height was another factor in attracting gifted draftsmen to the animation field. The Walt Disney Studio was one of the few places at the time where an artist could both earn a living and find challenging work to be done.

As the staff grew, so did the studio itself. In 1929 and 1930, additions had been made to the front, rear, and one side of the original Hyperion Avenue structure. In 1931, a two-story animation building was added. During a four-year period, the plant grew from 1,600 square feet of floor space to 20,000.

33

A 1931 theater marquee advertising Mickey Mouse

This still from *Mickey's Surprise Party*, 1939, a commercial made for the National Biscuit Company, shows that by the end of the decade Minnie had developed a certain nonchalant sophistication

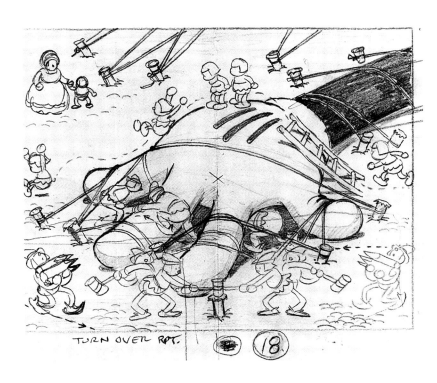

For *Playful Pluto*, 1934, Webb Smith devised and Norm Ferguson animated a scene in which Pluto becomes entangled with a strip of flypaper. A classic of its sort, this sequence demonstrates how Disney artists could take a simple situation and build on it in such a way that the humor arose directly from the personality of the character

Generally recognized as one of the classics of Disney animation, *The Band Concert,* 1935, was the first Mickey Mouse cartoon to be made in Technicolor. Mickey is discovered in the park of a small Midwestern town, directing an orchestra through a program of popular classics. He embarks on a spirited version of *The William Tell Overture,* but events conspire to disrupt the performance (left and below, a bee wreaks havoc). Most troublesome is Donald Duck, in the guise of a street vendor, who again and again leads the orchestra astray by playing "Turkey in the Straw" on an unending succession of fifes which are concealed about his person.

As the orchestra approaches the storm section of the overture, a more serious problem arises. A tornado, which seems to have been conjured up by the music, approaches the town. The twister picks up the entire orchestra - along with Donald, a farm house, and assorted vegetation - sending everyone and everything spinning in the air. Mickey holds the performance together by sheer will-power, and the piece comes to a rousing finale, with musicians hanging from trees and anything else that has been left standing.

It is interesting that the disruptive Duck plays Mickey's theme from *Steamboat Willie,* suggesting that Donald has taken over the role of mischief-maker from the Mouse

Gulliver Mickey, 1934, opposite middle, is one of several cartoons that make Mickey the hero of a children's classic

In *Orphan's Benefit,* 1934, opposite bottom, Donald Duck came into his own. His efforts to entertain a group of children are frustrated by the malicious behavior of the audience, which causes him to dissolve into helpless rage

3 Hyperion Days

In the 1930s, Walt Disney was the darling of artists and intellectuals, from writers such as H. G. Wells and Thornton Wilder, to filmmakers like René Clair and Sergei Eisenstein, to musicians as different as Arturo Toscanini and Jerome Kern.

"The two presiding geniuses of the movies are Walt Disney and Charlie Chaplin," declared Wilder. "Like Chaplin," added Wells, "[Disney] is a good psychologist and both do the only thing in film that remains international." "The reason [for the success of Disney and Chaplin]," said Clair, "is that they have no outside interference. They act as their own producer, director, and even attend to their own stories and musical scores. Their artistry is sublime."

The universality of Mickey Mouse was a frequent subject of comment. Harold Butcher, the New York correspondent for the *London Daily Herald,* wrote in 1934, "After a quick trip around the world . . . I have returned to New York to say that Mickey Mouse has been with me most of the way. On the Pacific, in Japan and China, at Manchouli – suspended precariously between Siberia and Manchukuo. . . ."

Given the high recognition factor that attached itself to Mickey and the other Disney characters, it is hardly surprising that the company's merchandising operation, headed by independent entrepreneur Kay Kamen, was by now a multimillion-dollar enterprise. *The American Exporter* informed its readers that "beside the 80 licensees in the U.S. who are manufacturing merchandise bearing the likeness of Mickey Mouse or some other of the Walt Disney characters, there are 15 in Canada, 40 in England, 80 on the European continent and 15 in Australia." *The New York Telegraph* reported in 1935 that total sales of Disney-licensed products would net $35,000,000 worldwide that year. Cartier offered a diamond bracelet bearing the likeness of Mickey for a mere $1,150. More significantly, both Lionel Trains and Ingersoll watches were virtually saved from bankruptcy by their Disney franchises. (Two million Mickey Mouse watches sold in a single eight-week period.)

Walt Disney had become a public figure and was learning to field the questions that come with fame. Always he seemed suitably

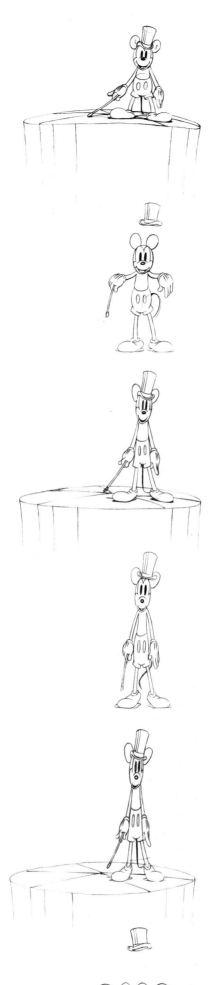

Mickey Mouse and Mary Pickford

Dick Lundy's animation drawings for
a sequence in which Mickey imper-
sonates Fred Astaire clearly show
how flexible Mickey's body had
become

Disney with Stan Laurel and Oliver Hardy

During the second half of the 1930s, Pluto became a star in his own right. This drawing is by Fred Moore

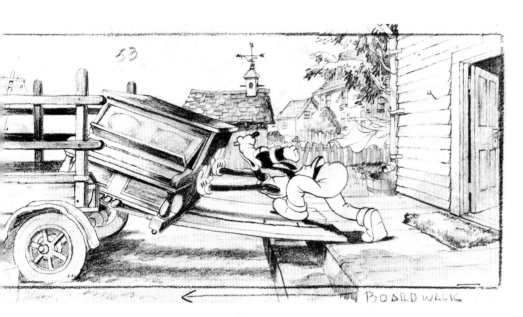

Moving Day, 1936, provides Goofy with some of his finest moments, pitting him against a piano with a mind of its own. This sequence, animated by Art Babbitt, is a sustained and inspired piece of nonsense. Comedy is distilled from the situation with a close regard for character that would have been unthinkable even two or three years earlier

Mickey's Circus, 1936, presented Mickey in a role that was a natural for him – the ringmaster

modest. "I do not draw, write music, or contribute most of the gags and ideas seen in our pictures today," he told *The New York Times.* "My work is largely to supervise, to select and shape material, to direct and coordinate the efforts of our staff."

Another reporter asked Disney how it felt to be a celebrity. "It feels fine," he replied, "when being a celebrity helps get a choice reservation for a football game.... As far as I can remember, being a celebrity has never helped me make a good picture, or a good shot in a polo game, or command the obedience of my daughter, or impress my wife. It doesn't even seem to help keep fleas off our dogs...."

So much for Disney the public figure, but what of the man who made the movies? How did his colleagues see him?

Jack Cutting, who joined the studio in the mid-thirties, recalled that Disney seemed mature beyond his years and, at times, very serious. "I always felt his personality was a little bit like a drop of mercury rolling around on a slab of marble because he changed moods so quickly. I believe this was because he was very sensitive.... He could grasp your ideas and interpret your thoughts rapidly. You didn't have to give Walt a five-page memo....

"Although Walt could exude great charm... he could also be dour and indifferent towards people – but this was usually because he was preoccupied by problems.... The people who worked best with Walt were those who were stimulated by his enthusiasm.... More than once, when he was in a creative mood and ideas were popping out like skyrockets, I have suddenly seen him look as if he had been hit in the face with a bucket of cold water. The eyebrow would go up and suddenly reality was the mood in the room. Someone in the group was out of tune with the creative spirit he was generating. Then he would say it was difficult to work with so-and-so."

Moose Hunters, **1937, presents Mickey, Donald, and Goofy in a series of typically disastrous confrontations with wildlife**

39

Studying penguins as an aid to animation: standing, left to right, Walt Disney, Albert Hurter, Leigh Harline, Frenchy de Trémaudan, Clyde Geronimi, Paul Hopkins (behind Geronimi), Hugh Hennesy, Art Babbitt, Norm Ferguson, and Bill Roberts. Seated, Dick Huemer and Wilfred Jackson

These creative moods were often exercised at the "sweatbox" sessions that were an essential part of the studio routine. (The projection rooms at Hyperion were not air conditioned, hence the name sweatbox.) As soon as a scene was animated, the drawings would be shot to create what was known as a pencil test. This would be run for Disney and the movie's creative team – director, story artists, animators – and the sequence under consideration would be subjected to a rigorous analysis in an effort to see if it could be improved. Sometimes, instead of a pencil test it would be a "Leica reel" that would be projected. Another Disney innovation, this consisted of still storyboard drawings synchronized to the sound track to give a rough idea of what would eventually be seen in theaters.

Another Disney veteran, Dick Huemer, was impressed by Walt's perspicuity on these occasions. "He always had the answers. He would go right to the middle of the problem and there would be this nugget that he'd pull

out. Damnedest thing! You'd kick yourself and say, 'Why didn't I think of that?'"

Marc Davis, master animator and one of the creative forces behind the Disney theme parks, was impressed from the first by Disney's readiness to gamble everything on an idea. "He was not afraid to risk every penny, go into hock, hire 150 people and wonder how he was going to meet the payroll. He did this all his life. He felt money is good only because of what you can do with it. Without him, I can't see animation having become much of a business. . . ."

As early as 1931, Disney had decided that his artists would benefit from further training, and he arranged for some of them to take an evening class at Chouinard Art School. This class was conducted by a young man called Don Graham, who was soon to have an important role in the Disney organization.

"In the fall of 1932," Graham later recalled, "Art Babbitt, one of the top animators at the studio, convinced Walt that instead of sending his men across town to Chouinard, it would be far wiser to conduct classes at the studio, where there could be more control of attendance. On November 15, 1932, the great Disney Art School was born in the old sound studio at Hyperion. First it was just two evenings a week, [but] in 1934 . . . the school changed its character completely. . . .

"At about this time, Walt announced his intention of making *Snow White*, which implied a vast expansion of the animation department. Early in 1935, he came to me and said, 'I need three hundred artists – get them.' And thus began a huge campaign of recruitment. . . . The new employees were brought to the studio in small groups, usually a dozen or so at a time. They were given from six to eight weeks to demonstrate their potential. . . . Usually I would work with them the first two weeks, every day, eight hours a day, utilizing a human model. Then their day would be devoted a half day to drawing, a half day to production problems. They were also encouraged to attend the evening school. . . ."

Walt Kelly, of *Pogo* fame, was a Disney artist for several years. In the drawing on the left he portrays, left to right, an invented character, himself, Ward Kimball, and Fred Moore. Caricature was practically a way of life at the studio

Several Disney shorts exploited caricature, *Mother Goose Goes Hollywood*, 1938, includes portraits of Katharine Hepburn and Laurel and Hardy

41

A scene from *Cock of the Walk*, 1935, a Silly Symphony which includes clever parodies of Hollywood dance routines

Many fine artists - Charles Philippi, Hugh Hennesy, Tom Codrick, and others - made layout drawings for Disney during the thirties. Their work often displays a high standard of draftsmanship, as in this example from *Thru the Mirror*, 1936

A 1935 background painting for
Mickey's Fire Brigade

Backgrounds for *Boat Builders*, 1938, above, and *Polar Trappers*, 1938, right

Typical of the kind of instructional material used was a book assembled by top animators Ted Sears and Fred Moore. This contained model sheets, indicating how characters should be drawn; photographs of humans and animals in action poses; and detailed personality analyses. The following, written by Sears, is a typical example:

"Mickey [Mouse] is not a clown . . . he is neither silly nor dumb.

"His comedy depends entirely upon the situation he is placed in.

"His age varies with the situation. . . . Sometimes his character is that of a young boy, and at other times, as in the adventure type of picture, he appears quite grown up. . . .

"Mickey is most amusing when in a serious predicament trying to accomplish some purpose under difficulties, or against time. . . . [The laughs] depend largely upon Mickey's expression, position, attitude, state of mind, etc., and the graphic way that these things are shown. . . ."

Before giving hints on how to draw the Mouse – "The body should be pliable at all times" – Fred Moore added his own thoughts on Mickey's personality:

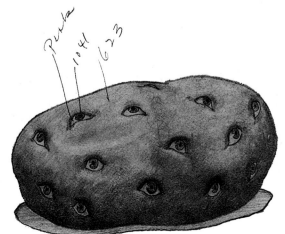

A layout drawing for *Mickey's Garden* (1935)

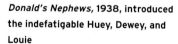

Donald's Nephews, 1938, introduced the indefatigable Huey, Dewey, and Louie

By the late thirties, Donald had all but eclipsed Mickey in popularity. Examples here are from two 1938 shorts, *Donald's Golf Game*, top, and *The Fox Hunt*, center. At bottom is one from the following year, *Donald's Cousin Gus*

After a cartoon was completed, story continuity drawings were stapled into books - often with surprising results. This group from *Fire Chief*, 1940, opposite, gives a marvelous sense of movement

Goofy in *Mickey's Amateurs*, 1937, above. The Goof's first solo outing was *Goofy and Wilbur*, 1939, left

"Mickey seems to be the average young boy of no particular age; living in a small town, clean living, fun loving, bashful around girls, polite and clever as he must be for the particular story. In some pictures he has a touch of Fred Astaire, in others of Charlie Chaplin, and some of Douglas Fairbanks, but in all of them there should be some of the young boy."

The fact that so much attention was being lavished on Don Graham's recruits did not mean that the veteran animators were ignored. As always, their work was subject to Walt Disney's personal attention, and as time passed he was becoming increasingly critical. This was not a matter of criticism for its own sake, however. Rather it was a way of attaining the standards that he perceived as necessary if the studio was to make the leap from eight-minute cartoons to feature-length films.

Spencer Tracy, Walt Disney, James Gleason, and Frank Borzage, at the old Riviera Polo Grounds.

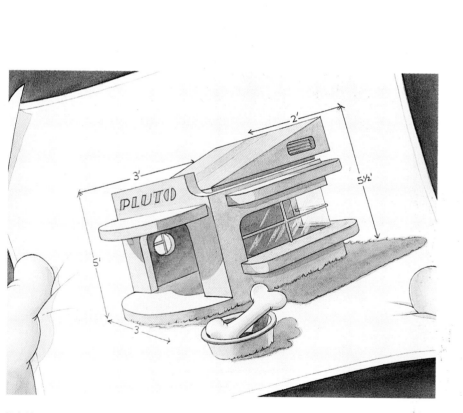

Painting for *Pluto's Dream House*, 1940

Given the level of activity maintained at the studio, it is amazing that anyone found time for leisure activities. In fact, a nearby vacant lot provided Disney employees with a playing field. Softball and volleyball games became popular lunchtime activities. Walt Disney seldom joined in these sports but, thanks to his friendship with Spencer Tracy, he did take up polo and even organized studio teams so that he and Roy could practice until they were good enough to join the movie colony teams that played at Will Rogers's Pacific Palisades estate and the old Riviera Polo Grounds.

Aside from family expeditions, polo seems to have been Walt Disney's only form of recreation at that time. Like the studio, the family was growing. By 1936, Walt and Lillian had two daughters, Diane and Sharon.

47

4 Five Animated Classics

The initial success of Mickey Mouse and the Silly Symphonies did not satisfy Disney for long, and as early as 1934 he began to think seriously about producing a feature-length animated film. One important consideration was purely practical. The Disney shorts were so popular that they often shared billing with the main feature, but because film rental was determined by running time the potential revenue from these shorts was inherently limited. Beyond this, Disney was anxious to work within an expanded format that would give him a chance to evolve more complex ideas and greater naturalism. In 1926, Max Fleischer had made an hour-long, partly animated film titled *Einstein's Theory of Relativity* that explained the theory, but nobody had made an animated feature that told a narrative story and could compete on equal terms with live-action movies. Most people in the industry thought it would be virtually impossible to do so. Who would sit still for eighty minutes of cartoon antics?

Cartoon antics were not what Walt Disney had in mind. He was planning to take a fairy story – Snow White and the Seven Dwarfs – and bring it to the screen with a kind of magic realism that was beyond the reach of live-action producers. (Interestingly, it is known that as a boy he had seen and been enchanted by a silent, live-action version of *Snow White*.) At first, he referred to his new project as the "Feature Symphony," and to some extent it can be seen as an extension of the Silly Symphony idea, because music still played a large part in the concept. But it was much more besides. No one can say just when Disney began to think seriously about *Snow White*, but by the summer of 1934 his thoughts were beginning to take concrete form. An exploratory outline, dated August 9 of that year, includes the following notes:

SLEEPY: Sterling Holloway. Falls asleep in midst of excitement, in middle of sentence, and so forth. . . .

Snow White sings as she washes the palace steps

"THE QUEEN" SNOW WHITE "PRINCE"

Early concept drawings for the
Queen, Snow White, and the Prince

Snow White

As *Snow White* went into production, Disney artists were asked how they thought the dwarfs might look and behave. These sketches are representative of the suggestions they made

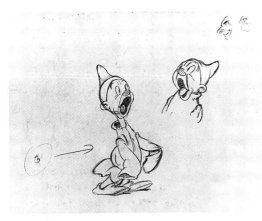

Albert Hurter's studies were vital to the concept of the story that began to emerge

HOPPY-JUMPY: Portrayed by Joe Twerp, the highly excitable, nervous radio comic who gets his words mixed up (flews nashes ry bichfield). He is in constant fear of being goosed but is not goosed until last scene.

BASHFUL: Portrayed by Buelow, a unique radio personality with a very funny bashful laugh. . . .

HAPPY: Portrayed by Professor Diddleton D. Wurtle, whose wild Ben Turpin eyes are reinforced by one of the funniest tricks of speech in radio. . . .

AWFUL: The most lovable and interesting of the dwarf characters. He steals the drinks and is very dirty. . . .

Anyone familiar with the finished movie will realize that the dwarfs were destined to go through many changes before they reached the screen, but we can see that their personalities were beginning to take shape. (None of the radio personalities named in the notes participated in the movie, but it is apparent that Disney was already aware of the importance voice talent would have in a feature movie.) This early manuscript also lists a number of

The opening scenes of *Snow White* establish the movie's theme and atmosphere with great economy. The Wicked Queen, her magic mirror, the Prince, and Snow White herself – little better than a servant in her stepmother's palace – are all introduced

Opposite:
A storyboard sketch shows the Queen transformed into a witch

such a way that, when the camera shot through the layers of glass, the elements seemed to relate to one another spatially as they would in real life.

Another consideration was that the Disney artists had very little experience in animating the human form. Toward the end of 1934, several animators were put to work on a Silly Symphony titled *The Goddess of Spring* that retold the Greek myth of Persephone. Thanks to Don Graham's art classes, the Disney artists had improved their knowledge of anatomy, but bringing the human form to life was still an elusive goal, and *The Goddess of Spring* proved that there was a long way to go before the studio could handle characters like Snow White and the Wicked Queen.

Over the next year or so, however, some of the better short cartoons demonstrated that the animators were beginning to achieve the standard that would be required. The carica-

tures of Hollywood personalities in a cartoon called *Broken Toys* were highly sophisticated, and Disney is said to have been especially happy with the way Jenny Wren's character was established in *Who Killed Cock Robin?* The studio's veteran animators were coming into their prime and younger artists were catching up fast.

Animators think of themselves as actors who perform with a pencil. The process of casting them for a production like *Snow White* was a sensitive one. In the end, the lineup of supervising animators read like a Who's Who of the top animation artists of two generations. Fred Moore, Vladimir (Bill) Tytla, Fred Spencer, and Frank Thomas were assigned to the dwarfs. (Moore's charm and Tytla's vigor would be needed for these characters; Spencer had a sure touch with broad comedy, and Thomas was one of the most promising of the younger artists.) The Queen, in her guise as an evil beauty, was given to Art Babbitt, while the

54

As Snow White flees into the forest,
trees and fallen logs become mon-
sters that seem to threaten her.
The Disney artists tried to see the
world through her frightened eyes,
turning it into a nightmare

The Queen entrusts her huntsman with the task of murdering Snow White. Once in the forest, however, he is overcome by the princess's innocence and drops to his knees to beg her forgiveness. Clever use of shadows and camera angles adds to the drama of the scene

Queen as the old witch was assigned to another veteran, Norm Ferguson. Three younger animators – Milt Kahl, Eric Larson, and Jim Algar – were put in charge of the animals who befriend Snow White. The heroine herself, the most crucial and difficult character of all, was consigned to Ham Luske and Grim Natwick – Luske was a specialist in character development, and Natwick was a superb draftsman with a strong knowledge of anatomy.

Casting Snow White's voice was almost equally tricky. Walt Disney was determined not to be influenced by the appearance of prospective voice talents. In order to retain his objectivity, he had a loudspeaker installed in his office so that he could hear singers auditioning on the soundstage without seeing them. Finally, Adriana Caselotti, a young woman with some opera training, was chosen.

By the spring of 1936, production of *Snow White* was in full swing. Story conferences were held almost every day, and each scene was analyzed down to the last detail. A stenographer was present at these meetings, and thus a complete record exists. Below, for example, is an excerpt taken from the transcript of a meeting held on the Hyperion soundstage on December 22, 1936.

Snow White is befriended by woodland creatures who take her to the dwarfs' cottage. Assisted by the animals, Snow White cleans the cottage and then – exhausted by her experience – falls asleep across several of the dwarfs' beds

Snow White was the only feature in which transparent colors were employed for the background paintings. Later, gouache became the usual medium

This drawing shows the attention to detail that informs every frame of *Snow White*

Twenty-nine people – mostly animators and animation directors – were on hand to discuss the dwarfs' personalities. The main feature of the meeting, which lasted from 7:00 P.M. to 10:20 P.M., was Walt Disney's detailed shot-by-shot description of the movie, a virtuoso performance as can be judged from this sample:

"We fade in on the sunset and hear the dwarfs coming home from the mine. They are marching home against the setting sun, singing the marching home song, which is the 'hiho' song that has the whistling chorus. We have a little sequence of these guys going over picturesque spots – mushrooms and roots of trees. There are little gag touches in there. We fade out on this sequence into the next sequence of Snow White, with a candle in her hand, and the animals following her upstairs. . . . She sees all these cute little beds, all seven, and she is pleased. These beds are hand carved and she reads the names on them, and she thinks they are little children. . . . Doc, Bashful, Grumpy, Dopey, Sneezy, Sleepy . . . and when she reads on to Sleepy she says, 'I'm a little tired myself,' and lies there on three beds and tries them all out. The animals see her get into bed and cover her up with a sheet as she goes to bed. The rabbits and deer and all the animals get in these beds and settle down for a snooze. You hear the offstage dwarfs singing the marching home song, and the animals dash and look out the window. They immediately scram out of the bedroom, run down out of the house, and hide. They anticipate these dwarfs coming. Then we pick up with the guys coming home, on up to Fred Moore's sequence where they come up to the bedroom to attack this monster."

The entire movie is described in this kind of detail, including two scenes that were later cut. What can be learned from this transcript is that *Snow White* existed in Walt Disney's head as a very concrete idea, and he was determined it should reach the screen exactly as he had conceived it. *Snow White* was a team effort, but it was still clearly the creation of one mind, and staff meetings were the medium through which Disney exercised his control over the

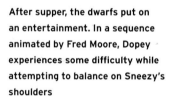

After supper, the dwarfs put on an entertainment. In a sequence animated by Fred Moore, Dopey experiences some difficulty while attempting to balance on Sneezy's shoulders

57

While Snow White sleeps, the dwarfs conclude their day's work at the mine and head for home, where they find the princess asleep on their beds

movie. They permitted him to keep everything under close scrutiny. The musical score was in the capable hands of Frank Churchill, Ollie Wallace, Leigh Harline, and Paul Smith, but Disney had his own ideas about how music should be used, as can be gathered from these comments from a meeting dated February 16, 1937:

"It can still be good music and not follow the same pattern everybody in the country has followed. We still haven't hit it in any of these songs. . . . It's still the influence from the musicals they have been doing for years. Really, we should set a new pattern – a new way to use music – weave it into the story so somebody doesn't just burst into song."

By the time *Snow White* reached the screen, its songs were indeed integrated with the story in a fresh and original manner. The way this was done anticipates the ingenuity with which Richard Rodgers and Oscar Hammerstein II incorporated songs into the

58

The dwarfs return to the lifeless body of Snow White and sadly place her in a crystal casket. She remains there through a full cycle of the seasons until, finally, the Prince arrives to wake her with a kiss

structure of *Oklahoma!*, which premiered in 1943. *Oklahoma!* was hailed as a breakthrough musical, but Disney had been moving toward the same goal several years earlier.

Capturing Snow White on screen was perhaps the biggest challenge of the movie. The problem with animating humans is that everyone in the audience instinctively knows how a man or a woman moves, and therefore the least inaccuracy in drawing is immediately apparent. By contrast, nobody has ever seen a "real-life" Mickey Mouse or a "real-life" Dopey, so the animator can invent freely. To assist the artists animating Snow White, live-action footage was shot using a young dancer, who would later achieve fame as Marge Champion. This yielded gestures and mannerisms that could never have been invented. The animators could have created Snow White by simply tracing the figures from photostats made from the frames of the live-action film – the process known as rotoscoping – but this was avoided since it tends to lead to stiff, unconvincing animation. Instead, the live-action footage was used strictly for reference purposes.

When animation of the heroine had been completed, and the cels came back from inking and painting, something was still missing. Snow White looked anemic. "She had no color in her cheeks," recalls Frank Thomas. "They tried painting color on there – which made her look like a clown. One of the [ink and paint] girls said, 'Walt, can we try putting a little rouge on her cheeks?' He said, 'What do you mean?' So she took out her makeup kit and put some rouge on the cel and it looked keen. Walt said, 'Yeah but how the hell are you going to get it in the same place every day? And on each drawing?' And the girl said, 'What do you think we've been doing all our lives?'... Without any kind of guide, they made Snow White up on each cel – so there's this lovely tint on there. That's how much we cared."

Although much of the production work on *Snow White* was jammed into the final ten

or twelve months, it was the result of more than three years of concentrated effort. From the very first, the whole venture had been an enormous gamble with almost the entire industry betting against its success. The staff of the Disney Studio had expanded to more than a thousand people, and finally, at a cost of close to $1,500,000, *Snow White and the Seven Dwarfs* was completed. Four days before Christmas, 1937, it premiered at the Carthay Circle Theater in Hollywood. The audience was studded with celebrities. It was the kind of opening night of which Disney had always dreamed. Better still, the film was greeted with rave reviews. *Snow White* was an overnight success, fulfilling all of Disney's hopes and impressing itself on the imagination of the world.

There may have been an element of luck in Disney's first great success with Mickey Mouse. *Snow White,* by contrast, was the result of a conscious and deliberate effort on his part to advance the art of animation to new levels of achievement – levels that everyone else had thought beyond reach.

Shirley Temple presents Walt Disney with a special Academy Award incorporating one large and seven little Oscars for his production of *Snow White*

Geppetto, delighted with his new son, sends Pinocchio off to school

Walt Disney in action: a sequence of photographs taken at a *Pinocchio* story conference

Many models were made to guide the animators

Pinocchio

One of Gustav Tenggren's watercolor
studies for *Pinocchio*

The release of *Snow White and the Seven Dwarfs* marked the beginning of an astonishing period of creativity on the part of the Walt Disney Studio. Between February of 1940 and August of 1942, four more Disney animated features were released. Each was destined to become a classic. It could be argued that the greatest of them – perhaps the greatest of all animated features to date – was *Pinocchio*.

The movie opens with a stunningly effective shot. The camera pulls back from a large white star, pans across the tiled roofs of a sleepy village, then closes in on the lighted window of Geppetto's cottage. It is the kind of shot that has since become familiar in live-action movies thanks to helicopters and power-operated zoom lenses. Within the context of its own period, however, it was innovative and spectacular. Nor was it just a piece of flashy showmanship. It served to draw audiences into the atmosphere of the story before a word was spoken. From that moment on, the film never loses its grip on the imagination.

Interestingly, *Pinocchio* did not get off to a good start. Perhaps buoyed by the success of his first feature, Disney embarked on this project less cautiously, putting the production into top gear before all the difficulties it presented had been solved. After six months, he was forced to call a hiatus. The primary dilemma centered on the character of Pinocchio himself. Should he be treated as a puppet or a small boy? Early animation had favored the puppet-like approach, but Disney was not satisfied with the results. After some experimentation, a more boy-like Pinocchio emerged (except in the scenes where he is still on strings).

Jiminy Cricket also presented a challenge. Because he is very small, he was difficult to animate except in close-ups. The animators rose to the occasion, making him so expansive that he seems larger than life.

In contrast to Jiminy Cricket stands one of the villains of the piece, the puppet master Stromboli. Animated by Bill Tytla, Stromboli is an enormous, muscular presence who fills the screen with his infamy, a man whose anger combines with his physical strength to keep him in a constant state of explosive agitation.

Also in the villains' camp are the fox and the cat – J. Worthington Foulfellow and Gideon – who are slyly determined to lead Pinocchio astray for the sake of a fast buck. Animated by Norm Ferguson and John Lounsbery, Foul-

The Blue Fairy rescues Pinocchio from the cage where Stromboli has locked him up, but not before he tells her a series of lies – only to discover that, with each lie, his nose grows longer and longer, eventually sprouting branches and leaves

fellow knows just when to throw a meaningful glance, and Gideon is a malicious dolt with an instinct for mischief.

Handled largely by Art Babbitt, Geppetto is the least interesting of the main characters, asked to function on a single, fundamentally sentimental level. Fred Moore was luckier with his assignment, treating Lampwick the cocky street kid as something of a self-caricature. Monstro the whale, animated by Wolfgang Reitherman, is suitably fearsome, and two small creatures, Figaro the kitten and Cleo the goldfish, add a touch of charm to the proceedings. Live action was shot as an assist to the animation of several characters, notably the Blue Fairy, whose brief appearances are very effective.

Layouts for *Pinocchio* are extremely inventive, and the background paintings are exceptionally fine. As in *Snow White*, Albert Hurter's influence is felt throughout the film, as is that of Gustav Tenggren, the gifted illustrator who made many inspirational studies for the project. Nor should the highly effective musical score be overlooked. It was less innovative, perhaps, than the score for *Snow White*, but it did its job well, highlighted by such songs as "Give a Little Whistle" and "When

62

A handsome layout drawing shows Jiminy Cricket in Geppetto's workshop

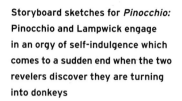

You Wish Upon a Star" – both composed by
Leigh Harline with lyrics by Ned Washington.

Pinocchio is a tour de force in which story
smarts and technical virtuosity are in perfect
balance. Reviewers welcomed it with enthusiasm, but it was not an immediate box-office
success. Its release came less than five months
after the outbreak of war in Europe, and perhaps the public was not in the mood for a fable
of this sort. Not that *Pinocchio* is a frivolous
movie; on the contrary, despite the happy ending, it presents the bleakest vision of any animated feature produced during Walt Disney's
lifetime, and it remains his masterpiece.

Pinocchio was produced mostly on the
old Hyperion lot. In August of 1939, about six
months before the movie opened, Disney
staffers began moving to a new studio on a
fifty-one-acre lot in Burbank, with buildings
designed by the distinguished Los Angeles
modernist Kem Weber and financed with the
profits from *Snow White.* The move was completed by the following spring, although a
skeleton staff remained at Hyperion for a couple of years more.

The undersea sequences in *Pinocchio* are spectacular and naturalistic, impressively so when it is realized that underwater photography was in its infancy at the time

Jiminy Cricket and the whale's eye

Escaping from the whale, who gives furious chase, Pinocchio is washed ashore, seemingly dead. The drama of the situation is here caught in storyboard sketches

The layout drawings for *Pinocchio* were made with great attention to detail. Often more than one artist worked on a single layout, the first making an outline drawing, and another adding the tonal rendering. Although never intended for public display, many of these drawings are very beautiful

The atmosphere of *Pinocchio* owed a great deal to the effectiveness of the background paintings

A storyboard sketch for the sequence in *The Sorcerer's Apprentice* where Mickey conducts the heavens

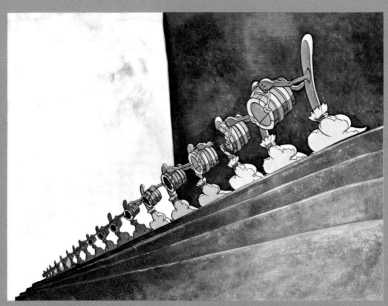

The Sorcerer's Apprentice presents Mickey as a neophyte magician dabbling with spells he cannot control. Mickey is at his most Chaplinesque, while the mindless robotlike force of the enchanted brooms and pails is reminiscent of the assembly-line machinery in *Modern Times* (1936)

Fantasia

A color sketch captures the moment
when the Sorcerer leaves Mickey
alone in the cavern. The Apprentice's
large shadow symbolizes his ambition

The emphasis on feature film production did
not mean Disney had lost his special affection
for Mickey Mouse, but Mickey continued to
lose ground to Donald in the popularity polls.
This prompted Disney to plan a comeback
for the Mouse. The vehicle he chose was *The
Sorcerer's Apprentice,* a folktale that Goethe
had employed as the basis for a popular poem.
Disney's immediate inspiration was Paul
Dukas's orchestral work of the same title, written in 1897. Anxious to lend the project as
much prestige as possible, Disney sought the
services of Leopold Stokowski, maestro of the
Philadelphia Orchestra. Stokowski had long
admired Disney's work and was delighted to
make himself available. He involved himself so
intensely in the development of the Mickey

project that it soon began to evolve into something far more ambitious, namely the feature
film *Fantasia,* which would be released in
November of 1940.

The idea that Disney and Stokowski settled
on was the production of what was originally
called "The Concert Feature," which would con-
sist of a recorded program of classical music
"illustrated" and enlivened by Disney animation.

The first thing to be decided upon was
the makeup of the program. Preliminary work
toward this end was done by Disney artists
Dick Huemer and Joe Grant (both music buffs)
in consultation with Stokowski and music
critic Deems Taylor. Eventually, the film was
broken down into seven main parts. The first
is an introduction, which culminates with

Disney artists transformed Tchaikovsky's *Nutcracker Suite* into a nature ballet featuring spectacular effects animation and delicate airbrush work

Stokowski's arrangement of Bach's *Toccata and Fugue in D Minor*. Next come excerpts from Tchaikowsky's *Nutcracker Suite*, then *The Sorcerer's Apprentice*, followed by Stravinsky's *Rite of Spring*. The fifth piece is Beethoven's Sixth Symphony, the "Pastoral." Next is "Dance of the Hours" from Amilcare Ponchielli's opera *La Gioconda*. The final section combines Mussorgsky's *Night on Bald Mountain* with Schubert's "Ave Maria."

The *Toccata and Fugue* segment of the movie was handed over to the studio's effects animation department, members of which took on the task of interpreting the patterns of Bach's music in terms of abstract and semiabstract forms. These forms often had more to do with the decorative aspects of Art Deco than with the more challenging achievements of artists like Kandinsky and Mondrian. Even so, this section of the movie is certainly adventurous considering the time in which it was made.

The *Nutcracker Suite* is ballet music, and Disney's artists treated this segment of the film as an animated dance suite, and each movement has its own character. One of the high spots of the entire movie is the "Chinese Dance" movement, animated with great wit,

In *Fantasia*, Stravinsky's *Rite of Spring* is used to underscore the story of the earth's prehistory, including the age of the giant reptiles

A pastel drawing for the "Pastoral"
segment. Such pre-production
studies are sometimes referred to
as "concept art"

Early studies for the "Pastoral"
segment of *Fantasia* betray influences
reaching back to the nineteenth-
century Symbolist movement

into the human condition. This segment of *Fantasia* is as fine as anything the Disney artists ever achieved.

Rite of Spring heralds an abrupt change of mood. Disney saw Stravinsky's ballet music as providing the score for nothing less than a portrayal of the creation of the world. This section of the movie begins with visions of a time when the world was still a molten mass and progresses through a schematic version of evolution till the dinosaurs are wiped out by a massive drought. The concept is interesting – especially in view of the fact that the Scopes trial, in which a science teacher was convicted for teaching evolution, was still a recent memory in 1941. On the whole, though, the execution is only intermittently interesting, making this the least successful part of *Fantasia*.

The next segment, set to the "Pastoral" symphony, has moments of charm yet seems decidedly lightweight for Beethoven's score, which can be explained by the fact that the Arcadian visuals were originally planned for a much slighter piece of music, an excerpt from Gabriel Pierné's *Cydalise*. This segment owes a great deal to the stylized decorative and illustrative idioms of the thirties. It passes before the viewer like an animated mural for

principally by Art Babbitt. A group of humorously choreographed mushrooms moves through a solemn routine with almost ritualistic motions. One, smaller than the rest, has great difficulty keeping up with his associates.

The Sorcerer's Apprentice is one of the high points of Mickey's career. He is presented as a young apprentice magician whose master leaves him with orders to clean the cavern where he practices his arcane craft. Donning the wizard's magic hat, Mickey is able to bring a broom to life and orders it to fill the cistern for him. Mickey then settles down to take a nap, dreaming of himself as "Master of the Universe." With no one to control it, the broom brings more and more water from the well, and when Mickey awakes he finds that the cavern is awash. He has no idea how to stop the broom, and when he tries to destroy it with an axe, it splits into many brooms that bring still more pails of water until the cavern is flooded. Just in time, the sorcerer returns to save the day. Chastened, Mickey is left to refill the cistern.

With this story, Mickey had certainly come a long way from *Steamboat Willie*. Although told in an amusing way, *The Sorcerer's Apprentice* presents psychological ideas that delve deeply

"Dance of the Hours," above and top left, as interpreted by the Disney artists, became a hilarious parody of classical ballet

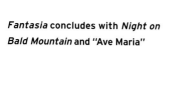

Fantasia concludes with *Night on Bald Mountain* and "Ave Maria"

some once fashionable restaurant. The best scene comes at the beginning when winged horses, like giant butterflies, glide in to make a graceful landing upon a lake. The high school jock centaurs and coed centaurettes are less successful, but good comic interludes are provided by Ward Kimball's Bacchus and his drunken unicorn-mule.

The segment ends as the goddess Diana appears in the night sky to launch an arrow of fire from the bow of light formed by the new moon. This leads into a very different section, "Dance of the Hours," in which the animators were given the task of developing a parody of classical ballet featuring unlikely dancers such as hippos, elephants, ostriches, and alligators. The results are hilarious, as gravity and reason are denied in a triumphant assault on conventional notions of grace.

Fantasia concludes with *Night on Bald Mountain* and "Ave Maria." Thanks to Bill Tytla's spectacular animation of Chernabog – a form of the Devil – the former is impressive. The latter is merely saccharine. In this respect, the

final segment reflects the values of *Fantasia* as a whole. It is a film with great merits and great faults. It broke new ground, but some of it might have been better left untilled. At times it is so crass as to be embarrassing, yet it remains an achievement that must be reckoned with.

Pinocchio and *Fantasia* were not moneymakers in their first release. Later, of course, they would find appreciative audiences, but in 1941 the studio needed to find a way of recouping the losses these astonishing movies had brought about. The answer proved to be a short, unpretentious, charming, and clever little film called *Dumbo*.

The tale of a flying elephant, *Dumbo* was found on the back of a cereal box. Disney story artists expanded this tale into a moving saga of a pachyderm youngster separated from his mother and driven to astonish the world by displaying the most unlikely of all talents.

After the demands of the first three features, working on *Dumbo* must have seemed like a vacation to the Disney artists. Clearly

71

Dumbo follows the career of a young elephant from the night he is delivered by stork at the winter quarters of the circus to the day he learns he can fly and to his "arrival" as a national celebrity. Along the way, he is befriended by a group of hipster crows. The movie includes a memorable sequence in which the hero's drunkenness offers an opportunity for some spectacular effects

Dumbo

they enjoyed themselves on this project, and the enjoyment is apparent on screen. *Dumbo* is probably the most spontaneous animated feature the Disney studio ever produced. There are few multiplane camera shots or elaborate special effects. This is just a good story, well told with a minimum of fuss. In many ways it is not unlike the great Disney short cartoons of the thirties, although on a larger canvas. Audiences responded to the picture with considerable enthusiasm, and the film's box-office success helped to alleviate the studio's financial woes.

Disney had other problems to deal with. By 1941, unionization had been firmly established in most of the Hollywood studios, but it had not made significant inroads into the animation industry. When picket lines were established outside the Disney lot – with employees demanding shorter hours and higher wages – Walt Disney was hurt and astonished. The dispute turned out to be bitter, and the wounds it left were deep. As a direct or indirect result of the 1941 strike, the studio lost some of its best animators, as well as much of the freewheeling atmosphere that had characterized it till then.

Some of the most inventive animation for *Dumbo* was done by Ward Kimball, who drew the hipster crows

Dumbo ends as the circus train carries the film's hero toward the bright lights of the big city

In *Bambi,* Disney artists aimed for a degree of naturalism quite unprecedented in the history of the animated film

Bambi and his father in the snow

Background treatments for *Bambi* were conceived to sustain a lyrical mood

Bambi

By coincidence, the theme of *Bambi* – the last of the five early classics – is the passing of a state of innocence: man invades the forest and brings terror and destruction to the creatures who live there. Work had begun on an adaptation of Felix Salten's book as early as 1937, before the release of *Snow White,* but for various reasons *Bambi* did not reach theaters until 1942. By its very nature, it was a project that could not be rushed, and the studio's financial problems slowed things down. While *Fantasia* ate up the company's resources, *Bambi* was cut back to a skeleton crew and did not return to full-scale production until *Fantasia* was finished.

Bambi tells the story of a deer growing to maturity in the forest. His mother is killed by hunters, but he has animal friends such as the rabbit Thumper. Despite comic interludes, the prevailing mood of this film (at least until the climax) is one of lyricism. The forest itself becomes a character in the movie, every bit as important as any of the animals. Much of the credit for this should go to Tyrus Wong, who keyed the background styling.

Great emphasis was placed on naturalism. Special art classes were instituted to instruct the animators in drawing live animals, which were brought to the studio. Books of photographic studies and innumerable model sheets were compiled, along with expert analyses of animal action and thousands of feet of live-action footage shot for reference in the Maine woods.

Much patient work went into the making of *Bambi*, and it is worth singling out the contributions of the art direction team, headed by Tom Codrick, along with the animation of Frank Thomas, Milt Kahl, Ollie Johnston, Eric Larson, and Retta Scott. The movie has undeniable flaws, but it should be acknowledged that *Bambi* took animation in a direction no one but Disney would have dared take it, and, for all its faults, it succeeds in creating a world that is totally engaging. In order to understand just how remarkable an achievement this was, it is important to remember that barely five years before it was completed no one had ever seen a feature-length animated movie, let alone one that took on such a difficult theme and handled it with such flair and imagination.

As things turned out, *Bambi* marked the end of an era. The expansion that had begun in the early thirties reached its peak and leveled off around 1940. By the time *Bambi* reached the screen, America was fully involved in World War II, and the armed forces were depleting the studio's ranks. In addition, the Depression conditions that had made so many artists available in the thirties had become a thing of the past. It was a time for regrouping. For a while, the Walt Disney studio would have to coast – capitalizing on its past achievements, working well within its known capabilities, experimenting a little, and waiting for energies to be restored.

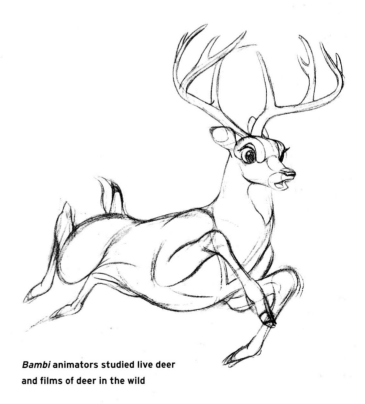

***Bambi* animators studied live deer and films of deer in the wild**

5 Interruptions and Innovations

America's entry into World War II had an almost immediate effect on Walt Disney Productions. In December 1941, part of the Burbank studio was commandeered as quarters for an antiaircraft unit which stayed for several months. Before long, the government and the armed services realized that animation could be of great value in the presentation of training and propaganda material, and Disney artists were soon producing films with titles such as *Aircraft Carrier Landing Signals* and *Food Will Win the War*. A more ambitious project, financed by Walt Disney himself, was *Victory Through Air Power*, a feature-length film presenting the strategic bombing theories of Major Alexander de Seversky.

Throughout the war, the studio continued to produce Donald, Pluto, and Goofy shorts. (Mickey was temporarily shelved in 1942.) Some of these were geared to the war effort. *Victory Vehicles*, for example, used Goofy to encourage Americans to conserve rubber and gasoline, while *Der Fuehrer's Face*

took the form of a nightmare in which Donald found himself trapped in a hellish Nazi world.

The two most important commercial releases of the period were themselves indirect products of the war. With Europe in turmoil, Latin American markets became increasingly important to Hollywood filmmakers, and in 1941, with government sponsorship, Disney and a team of artists traveled to Argentina, Peru, Chile, and Brazil. Each of these countries formed the background for an animated short and these four episodes were connected with documentary footage of the tour to create a "package" or "anthology" film released in 1943 as *Saludos Amigos*. The most memorable character to emerge from this movie was José Carioca, the samba-loving parrot who would reappear two years later in *The Three Caballeros*, another Latin-accented package film that matched him with Donald and a trigger-happy Mexican rooster named Panchito.

The package film was not an ideal format for the Disney artists, but it was a way of putting

During World War II, Disney characters were often used to illustrate matters of public interest. In *Victory Vehicles*, 1943, Goofy urged people to save scrap metal and gasoline

The 1943 package film *Saludos Amigos* included the story of Pedro the mail plane and introduced Donald's friend José Carioca

The animated portions of *Song of the South*, 1946, brought the animals of the Uncle Remus stories to life

together a feature-length release at a time when wartime shortages and economic pressures made true features impractical. Some of these pressures continued after the war and three more package films were released in three years – *Make Mine Music* (1946), *Fun and Fancy Free* (1947), and *Melody Time* (1948). Another money-saving approach was the live-action/animation hybrid: in *Song of the South*, cartoon creatures ocasionally intruded into the live action, and fully animated segments brought to life Brer Rabbit and other characters from the Uncle Remus stories. These animated segments represent the best work done by Disney artists during this period of transition.

By 1949, the studio was almost ready to return to true feature animation and that year saw the release of *The Adventures of Ichabod and Mr. Toad*, a package made up of two longish "featurettes." The Toad episode is based on Kenneth Grahame's *The Wind in the Willows*, and despite some subpar animation, there are hints of what Disney could have done with this wonderful material if it had been expanded to full feature length. The studio's version of the tale of Ichabod, based on Washington Irving's *The Legend of Sleepy Hollow*, is notable mainly for the outstanding and scary final sequence in which Ichabod is pursued by the Headless Horseman.

The Disney studio was still producing short cartoons for theatrical release and continued to do so until 1956. Donald and Goofy were now the big stars, and Mickey made only occasional appearances. Important new characters were Chip and Dale, the highly territorial chipmunks who knew how to make Donald's life miserable. Donald's nephews – the irrepressible Huey, Dewey, and Louie – also made frequent appearances. Besides the cartoons

Donald Duck appears in *Slide Donald Slide*, 1949, above. Much fine work went into the short cartoons of the forties, as in the example of a background, left

Cinderella was Disney's first true animated feature since *Bambi*. Released in 1950, it recaptured much of the spirit of the early features, modified by a new lightness of touch and an emphasis on surface glamour

Cinderella

featuring these "standard" characters, Disney also produced one-shot shorts such as *Morris the Midget Moose* (1950) and *Susie the Little Blue Coupe* (1952). In a sense, these were replacements for the Silly Symphony series that had been abandoned before the war. On occasion, short subjects were accorded special treatment, as was the case with *Toot, Whistle, Plunk and Boom* (1953), a highly stylized history of music and the first cartoon to make use of the CinemaScope® format.

Earlier, in 1950, Walt Disney released his first full-length animated film in eight years. This was *Cinderella* – a project that had been in development for several years – and it was a success both at the box office and as a piece of imaginative filmmaking. In spirit, it harks back to *Snow White and the Seven Dwarfs*, although with an added frosting of surface glamour and a greater reliance on gag routines. Cinderella, her stepmother, and the Prince are treated somewhat naturalistically, whereas Cinderella's Fairy Godmother, the Ugly Sisters, the King, and the Duke are presented as caricatures, but all mesh well together. The animals of the subplot are brilliantly conceived, especially Lucifer the cat, who makes a fine villainous partner to the wicked stepmother.

The backgrounds for *Cinderella* are less distinctive than those which added so much to *Snow White* and *Pinocchio*, but they are more than adequate. The songs, which include "So This Is Love" and "A Dream Is a Wish Your Heart Makes," are up to Disney's established high standards. In the end, *Cinderella* succeeds because it remains faithful to the spirit of the original fairy tale, while embroidering it with the kind of touches Disney understood better than anyone else. The next feature, *Alice in Wonderland* (1951), failed because it neither captures the unique atmosphere of Lewis Carroll's

Cinderella's Fairy Godmother prepares her for the ball

81

Disney's version of *Peter Pan*, 1953, is a generally entertaining interpretation of Sir James Barrie's stage classic

with until then: something rather close to our everyday world, the suburbs of a medium-sized American city in the early years of the twentieth century. Indeed, it is a setting such as Walt Disney must have known when he was delivering newspapers as a boy. The story of the relationship between Lady – a pedigreed dog born to the good things in life – and Tramp – a mutt from the wrong side of the tracks – is strong and beautifully told. The Disney artists did a fine job of grafting human personas onto the principal canine characters, without losing the nuances of dog behavior that were necessary for the movie to be convincing. There were technical problems to be faced as well. The elongated CinemaScope format meant that no one character could dominate a shot in close-up and characters had to be grouped in new and looser ways so that there would be no dead patches on screen. The layout team handled this challenge with great flair and, along with *Cinderella*, *Lady and the Tramp* must be considered one of the two best animated features of the 1950s.

story nor displays the authoritative Disney style except in a few isolated scenes, such as the Mad Hatter's tea party, which show flashes of sharp surrealistic invention. Ultimately, Disney failed to find a cinematic equivalent for Carroll's witty and erudite word games. Disappointed with the film, he blamed its failure on the heroine's "lack of heart."

Peter Pan, released in 1953, is an altogether more satisfactory picture – and provides a demonstration of just how expert the Disney animators had become at handling the human form. Sir James Barrie's play adapted well to the screen. If the movie has a weakness, it derives from the fact that there are too many characters to permit all of them to be developed adequately in the seventy-seven-minute running time. Character development apart, though, the movie has a satisfying narrative flow, well-handled comedy routines, and more than its fair share of magic moments in which the art of animation makes the impossible possible.

The year 1955 saw the release of *Lady and the Tramp*, Disney's first animated feature in CinemaScope. The story takes place in a milieu that Disney feature animation had not dealt

Released in 1951, *Alice in Wonderland* had some brilliant visual touches but failed to capture the flavor of Lewis Carroll's story

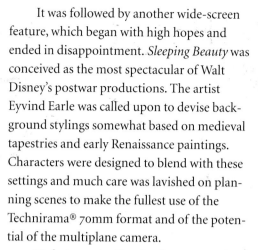

It was followed by another wide-screen feature, which began with high hopes and ended in disappointment. *Sleeping Beauty* was conceived as the most spectacular of Walt Disney's postwar productions. The artist Eyvind Earle was called upon to devise background stylings somewhat based on medieval tapestries and early Renaissance paintings. Characters were designed to blend with these settings and much care was lavished on planning scenes to make the fullest use of the Technirama® 70mm format and of the potential of the multiplane camera.

Unfortunately, *Sleeping Beauty* went into production at a time when Disney was preoccupied with live-action films and especially with Disneyland. The movie has some good moments – Maleficent, animated by Marc Davis, is a wonderful villain – but the hero and heroine are ciphers who often seem to be lost against the overelaborate and overstylized backgrounds. Disney's storytelling sense and cinematic know-how are only intermittently present. Lacking a strong sense of direction, the movie took six years to complete and when it finally reached theaters, in 1959, it was greeted with negative reviews.

Released in 1955, *Lady and the Tramp* was the first animated feature made in CinemaScope. More significantly, it broke new ground in terms of subject matter, setting a more informal tone for future Disney movies

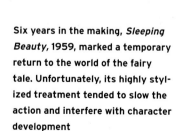

Six years in the making, *Sleeping Beauty*, 1959, marked a temporary return to the world of the fairy tale. Unfortunately, its highly stylized treatment tended to slow the action and interfere with character development

One Hundred and One Dalmatians, 1961, was the first feature to use the Xerox camera - a device which gave the backgrounds a more linear and graphic quality and helped preserve the spontaneity of the animator's drawings. This film provides fast-moving entertainment and a classic villain, Cruella De Vil, opposite bottom, one of the most memorable Disney characters of the postwar era

One Hundred and One Dalmatians

The next feature, *One Hundred and One Dalmatians* (1961), was made for a more conventional aspect ratio screen. Xerox photography was used to transfer the animators' drawings directly onto cels without being traced by inkers. This technology was devised by Ub Iwerks, who had returned to the studio in 1940 as head of special processes. The method would be used for the next three decades and it dictated a very graphic approach to animation with an emphasis on linear qualities.

Without the Xerox camera, *One Hundred and One Dalmatians* would have been impossible, or at least impractical, to make. There are scenes in which dozens of puppies – each liberally spotted – literally fill the screen. The Xerox system allowed the artists to animate one small group of puppies, then use the camera to repeat these actions, staggered in such a way that the repeats are not perceptible.

Set in England, the movie starts a little slowly but comes vividly to life when Cruella De Vil – another of Marc Davis's delicious delinquents – enters the picture, determined to acquire a coat made from Dalmatian puppy pelts. The pace picks up and never flags, as the story builds steadily to its satisfying climax.

Some of the most interesing animation in the movie was reserved for the humans, who were drawn with a looseness new to Disney

Cruella's mansion was one of the inspirations for the Haunted Mansion at Walt Disney World

features. Elbows and knees are not always where they should be according to anatomy books, but everything works. Cruella is especially memorable, her face a blend of death mask and fashion plate, perfectly expressing her character, which is at the same time evil and laughable. With *One Hundred and One Dalmatians*, the studio recovered much of its old assurance and arrived at a new idiom. Interestingly, Walt Disney is said to have strongly disliked the look of the movie. But the public approved and made the film a resounding commerical success.

The Sword in the Stone was not one of the studio's better efforts. Released in 1963, this film presents the boyhood of King Arthur, concentrating on his education at the hands of Merlin the Magician. Sadly, the production misses the spirit of T. H. White's original story. There are a few amusing set pieces but, instead of being an awesome figure, Merlin is shown as a bungling nincompoop, thus destroying the essence of the plot.

The Jungle Book, which appeared four years later, works much better. Based on Rudyard Kipling's tales about Mowgli, a human child brought up as a wolf cub in the jungles of India, the movie takes liberties with the original, but these are amply justified by the end results.

Voice talents – including George Sanders, Phil Harris, Louis Prima, Sterling Holloway, and Sebastian Cabot – played an important part in the production of *The Jungle Book,* 1967. This adaptation of Kipling's stories also features some of the best animation of the period

Part of the film's success derives from the skillful casting of voice talent. The voices of Sterling Holloway, Louis Prima, Verna Felton, and Sebastian Cabot are all used to good effect, but the show is stolen by Phil Harris (Baloo the Bear) and George Sanders (Shere Khan the tiger). The movie also features fine character animation and the best backgrounds in years, produced under the supervision of veteran Al Dempster.

Tragically, *The Jungle Book* turned out to be Walt Disney's last animated film. Several months before it was finished, in the fall of 1966, a routine medical exam revealed that

Disney – a heavy smoker – was suffering from advanced lung cancer. One lung was removed, but six weeks later, on December 15, he died in his room at St. Joseph's Hospital in Burbank, directly across the street from the studio he had built. He was sixty-five years old.

Before he died, Walt Disney had given the go-ahead for the studio's next animated feature, which appeared in 1970 as *The Aristocats.* This film blended the vernacular style of *One Hundred and One Dalmatians* with *The Jungle Book*'s developments in voice characterization, and the result is a slight but beautifully crafted comedy that enjoyed considerable popularity.

A blue-blooded cat named Duchess (her voice supplied by Eva Gabor) and her three kittens become the objects of the evil designs of their mistress's butler. Stranded in the French countryside, they are befriended by an alley cat named O'Malley (Phil Harris again). The film follows their adventures as they make their way back to Paris, only to be confronted once more by the blackhearted majordomo. This time, the villain gets his just deserts and Duchess and O'Malley live happily ever after.

Winnie the Pooh and the Honey Tree (1966) is a featurette made while Walt Disney was still alive. Apart from the unnecessary Americanization of some of A. A. Milne's characters, the Disney artists dealt well with translating the original Christopher Robin stories to the screen. They did even better in 1968 when a team of animators led by Frank Thomas, Ollie Johnston, John Lounsbery, and Milt Kahl was let loose on a second Milne featurette, *Winnie the Pooh and the Blustery Day.* Highlighted by Kahl's brilliant interpretation of Tigger, and Johnston's scenes in which Piglet is blown away like a kite in a hurricane, this is an example of Disney animation at its best. Almost as good is *Winnie the Pooh and Tigger Too* (1974). Later, these three featurettes were combined to make a feature, *The Many Adventures of Winnie the Pooh.*

Released in 1973, *Robin Hood* was designed from the first as a feature and must be considered one of the minor examples of the genre. There is nothing seriously wrong with this movie; it features some excellent character animation and amusing comedy situations, but it is an instance of the parts holding up quite well while the whole is somehow less than satisfying. Walt Disney's story sense is all too obviously lacking.

Almost four years passed before another animated feature appeared, and this time it was *The Rescuers*, based on stories by Marjory Sharp. The plot involves Bianca and Bernard (the voices of Eva Gabor and Bob Newhart), a pair of noble-hearted mice who set out to rescue a young orphan from the clutches of a suitably avaricious villain named Madame Medusa (Geraldine Page). This is not one of the studio's greatest animated stories, but it is a lively entertainment full of colorful characters and situations, a movie that has an honorable place in the Disney oeuvre. It is also a transitional movie in that it was made under the guidance of the old guard – the men who had been there since *Snow White* – but was the first feature to display a significant influence from the next generation of Disney artists. The list of character animators includes names like Ron Clements, Glen Keane, and Andy Gaskill, who would have significant roles to play in the animation renaissance of the eighties and nineties.

This changing of the guard was even more in evidence by the time of *The Fox and the Hound* (1981). Veteran Woolie Reitherman

A scene from *The Aristocats*, 1970, which featured a villainous butler and strong comic relief

was the producer, and Frank Thomas and Ollie Johnston did much of the developmental work on the main characters. Most of the actual animation, however, was in the hands of a youthful team that included Clements, Keane, and John Musker. Others listed in the credits for this movie were Don Hahn (assistant director) and Burny Mattinson (story), both of whom, like the artists listed above, would be of great importance to the future of Disney animation.

The story of Tod and Copper, who grow up as friends, only to find that they are expected to hate one another, *The Fox and the Hound* is a good example of middle-period Disney feature animation. The movie is full of solid characters and is enlivened by some strong action footage, notably the climactic confrontation between Tod and a bear animated by Glen Keane with a power reminiscent of Bill Tytla.

Starring Tigger, Eeyore and, of course, Pooh Bear, *Winnie the Pooh and the Blustery Day,* **1968, is a charming featurette-length adaptation of an A. A. Milne story**

The Fox and the Hound

Amos Slade's shack: one of the settings used for *The Fox and the Hound*

Based on stories by Margery Sharp, *The Rescuers,* 1977, is a lively adventure yarn which once again benefits greatly from the voice talents employed, notably Eva Gabor (Miss Bianca), Bob Newhart (Bernard), and Geraldine Page (Madame Medusa)

Good as *The Fox and the Hound* is, the younger generation of artists needed to escape from the imposing shadow of their elders. Their opportunity appeared to have arrived when Ron Miller – Walt Disney's son-in-law, who was the head of production – gave the go-ahead for *The Black Cauldron,* to be based on the Lloyd Alexander books that make up his popular "Chronicles of Prydain" cycle. This was a project calculated to capture the imagination of a youthful male audience, and in retrospect it is easy to see why it was embraced so eagerly by young artists eager to make a name for themselves. They had little difficulty in immersing themselves in the adventures of Taran and Eilonwy as they pitted their wits against the evil forces of the Horned King. Free of the supervision of the generation of the nine old men, the new Disney artists were making a movie entirely for themselves.

That may have been where the problems started. By the time they ended, the studio was under new management.

89

6 New Beginnings

At the time *The Black Cauldron* went into production, the Disney studio was desperately seeking a new sense of direction and purpose that would allow it to thrive in the 1980s. To compete with other studios, it needed to reach segments of the market it had not yet tapped. The Disney name could actually be a liability because it was so exclusively identified with the family market; young adults tended to stay away from Disney films. It was hoped that *The Black Cauldron* would be a partial answer to this problem. Unfortunately, the film proved to be a disaster.

This was not for lack of talent. Gifted young artists – many of them trained at the California Institute of the Arts, a school that has been generously endowed by the Disney family – were flocking to the studio. The problem was that no leadership remained when the old guard left. Despite the presence of accomplished newcomers like Tim Burton, Andreas Deja, John Lasseter, and Ruben Aquino, the production lacked direction. It was, in fact, divided up among several different units, some of which hardly communicated with one another as individuals battled for power. One splinter group – led by two story department veterans (Burny Mattinson and Dave Michener) and two relative newcomers (John Musker and Ron Clements) – actually broke away from *The Black Cauldron* and began working on another project tentatively titled *Basil of Baker Street*.

As *The Black Cauldron* limped toward completion, the studio itself was plunged into turmoil, as various management and shareholder alliances battled for control of the company. Eventually, in the fall of 1984, a new corporate team took the reins, with Michael Eisner (former president of Paramount Pictures) as chairman and Frank Wells (former vice chairman of Warner Brothers) as president of what would soon be renamed The Walt Disney Company. This was by far the biggest break with continuity in the company's history, but it by no means completely severed ties with the Disney family: the new leadership had the strong backing of Roy E. Disney, son of Roy O. Disney and nephew of Walt, who threw his support to the Eisner/Wells team on the understanding that they would give the animation program a chance to prove itself. Eisner backed up his promise by appointing Disney head of the feature animation department. Many insiders believe this decision saved the department and paved the way for the animation renaissance of the eighties and nineties.

Another of Eisner's first executive acts was to make Jeffrey Katzenberg – former head of production at Paramount – the chairman of Walt Disney Pictures. He too would have an influence on the way Disney animation evolved over the next several years.

By this time, *The Black Cauldron* was almost ready for release, and both Katzenberg and Roy Disney took their first look at the production reel. "I had heard there were problems," says Roy Disney, "but I wasn't prepared for what I saw. I looked at it and I knew we were in deep trouble."

Katzenberg had much the same reaction. The story was relentlessly bleak, and by the halfway point it began to meander aimlessly toward a wholly unsatisfactory ending. Calling on his live-action experience, Katzenberg took over the twenty-five-million-dollar production and headed for the editing room. The idea

The Black Cauldron

A critical and commercial disaster, *The Black Cauldron* is a film that most of those involved with its making would like to forget. Despite its very evident shortcomings as a narrative, however, *The Black Cauldron* did display a high level of ambition that signaled the aspirations of the new generation of Disney animators

of editing an animated film after it has been completed is considered virtual sacrilege, but Katzenberg felt he had no alternative. "We had to get in there with a scalpel," he says, and he did succeed in cutting two or three minutes from the film, but it was too late to alter the overall concept. Released in the summer of 1985, *The Black Cauldron* received generally unfavorable reviews and did poor business. It was finally re-released on video in 1998. Despite its problems, it remains a watershed in the Disney canon if only because it represents an elevation of ambition on the part of the younger artists.

A blow to the animators' pride came when the new regime moved them out of the hallowed Burbank animation building, where almost all of the classics had been produced, and into a Glendale industrial park, a couple of miles away. Still, the promise made to Roy Disney held firm, and he and Katzenberg took a look at the storyboards that had been produced by the splinter group working on *Basil of Baker Street*. They liked what they saw and responded with cautious enthusiasm.

"What Jeffrey said," recalls John Musker, "was, 'If you can make it in half the time you're used to, for half the money – go ahead.'"

A gentle spoof of Sherlock Holmes stories, the project was retitled *The Great Mouse Detective* and was produced on budget and in time to be released just a year after *The Black*

When Michael Eisner became chairman of the Walt Disney Company, he set about reorganizing the studio and transformed it into an entertainment industry giant

Cauldron. Far less ambitious than its predecessor, it is a very successful movie within its carefully drawn limitations – an entertaining film that pays tribute to earlier Disney masterpieces, while pointing the way to triumphs still to come. It is enlivened by some excellent character animation and displays an emphasis on story that Walt Disney would have approved of. The movie is full of snappy dialogue and witty sight gags – the latter sometimes more reminiscent of vintage Warner Brothers cartoons than of anything found in the Disney archive. It also contains one memorably spectacular sequence, partly computer animated, in which the hero and villain dodge flywheels and counterweights in the clocktower of London's Houses of Parliament.

The Great Mouse Detective was well received and turned a respectable profit. A modicum of pride had been restored to the feature animation department, and new projects were put into development.

Made on a low budget, *The Great Mouse Detective*, 1986, proved to be a lively entertainment with strong characters and plenty of humor well integrated into the plot. It demonstrated that Disney feature animation was over its crisis and headed in the right direction

They would come under the eye of Peter Schneider – a young man with a strong theater background – who had been recruited to run the department on a day-to-day basis. This was a crucial appointment because it provided the hands-on leadership that had been missing. Schneider's theatrical instincts were felt at story meetings, but beyond that he became the person who adjudicated disputes, made difficult decisions, appointed personnel to key positions, soothed sore egos, and generally kept the wheels oiled so that the animators and other artists could get on with making movies to the best of their abilities.

While this was happening in California, an astonishing Disney project was getting under way in London. The studio owned film rights to Gary K. Wolf's 1981 book *Who Censored Roger Rabbit?* and the new management team was intrigued by the possibility of a movie in which human actors and cartoon characters consort together in a never-never land version of Los Angeles. They passed the idea on to Steven Spielberg, who was fascinated but said he would become involved only if he could be guaranteed that the interaction between live-action footage and animation would be seamless and completely naturalistic. In earlier films (*Mary Poppins* for example) the live-action footage had always been shot with a locked-off camera, which is anchored to the floor and unable to move. This simplified the task of combining the diverse elements, but it led to stilted filmmaking. Spielberg insisted that *Who Framed Roger Rabbit* (as the film came to be called) would have to be made without sacrificing camera movement and flexibility. Also, he wanted to see cushions that sagged beneath the imaginary weight of cartoon characters and other instances of interactive naturalism that would make it believable that "toons" could visit our world and that humans could visit Toontown.

Who Framed Roger Rabbit, 1988, is an astonishing tour de force in which an international team of animators, led by Richard Williams, invented new ways to combine animation with live action so that director Robert Zemeckis could use his actors as flexibly as he would in an all live-action film. In this scene, Roger takes a ride with Eddie Valiant (Bob Hoskins)

Here, live-action Eddie Valiant encounters Jessica Rabbit, who is animated in every sense of the word

Who Framed Roger Rabbit

No more of a cartoon than some Hollywood actresses of the 1940s and 1950s, Jessica is pivotal in the artful balancing act that permits animated and live action characters to interact. As the Ink & Paint Club's resident chanteuse, she leaves toons swooning and human customers thoroughly confused

Traveling in their vintage Black Maria, Judge Doom's weasel sidekicks terrorize Toontown

Robert Zemeckis was selected to direct the movie and he traveled to London to meet with the legendary, Canadian-born animation director Richard Williams. Williams expressed strong misgivings about the project but finally told Zemeckis he thought the film could be made – if they threw the rule book out. Zemeckis should go ahead and shoot the movie the way he would shoot any movie, with fluid camera movements that did not take the animators' problems into account. Then it would become the animation crew's responsibility to make the cartoons fit into the live-action continuum.

The process involved was somewhat as follows. Scenes were storyboarded as they are for an animated movie. These boards were used as a guide for building sets and props and as a guide to directing the live performers (who had to pretend they were interacting with the "toon" characters). Photostats were made of each frame of live-action film and these were then used as layouts to guide the animators.

Not that it was quite that simple, because the animation had to be meshed with physical effects and somewhat complicated behavior on the part of the human performers. (Think of the scenes in which Roger and Eddie Valiant, played by Bob Hoskins, are handcuffed together.) Far from making things easy, the Williams team deliberately set itself technical problems with the idea of emphasizing the interaction between live action and animation, believing that this added to the sense of reality.

Who Framed Roger Rabbit not only introduced several new "toon" characters – including Roger himself, Jessica, Baby Herman, Benny the Cab, and a gaggle of weasely bad guys – it also called on the services of a score of old Disney favorites, from Clara Cluck to Tinker Bell, and cartoon stars such as Bugs Bunny and Woody Woodpecker on loan from other studios. An astonishing technical tour de force, *Roger Rabbit* is also an exceptionally coherent and entertaining film, and it enjoyed a great deal of well-deserved box-office success when it was released in 1988. Much of the credit

should go to Zemeckis, who handled the film with a suitably deft touch, and to the human actors, especially Bob Hoskins. Still, it would be impossible to overstate the contribution of Richard Williams and his animation crew, who made *Roger Rabbit* the unique cinematic experience it is.

Although fiercely independent, Williams had been a lifelong admirer of the Disney school of animation, maintaining a close relationship over the years with men like Milt Kahl, Frank Thomas, Ollie Johnston, Art Babbitt, Bill Tytla, and Grim Natwick. This was Williams's opportunity to make his own idiosyncratic contribution to the canon, and he made the most of it.

Aside from its intrinsic merit, *Roger Rabbit* was also very important for the future of Disney animation. Its success helped reestablish a bond, in the mind of moviegoers, between the Disney name and truly inventive animation. It could not have come along at a better time.

Disney's next all-animated film was *Oliver & Company* (1988), derived from Charles Dickens's *Oliver Twist*. In this story, set in New York City, Oliver was recast as an orphan kitten, while various other characters, including the Artful Dodger, were turned into dogs. A lively movie, if not especially memorable, *Oliver & Company*

Oliver & Company, 1988, made a good deal of use of computer-generated animation, employed to create elements such as automobiles and urban landscapes

Ariel rescues Eric

The Little Mermaid was marked by art direction reminiscent of Disney animation's first golden age. Also featured were strong supporting characters such as Sebastian, left, and a larger-than-life villainess in the person of Ursula the sea witch, below

The Little Mermaid

is noteworthy because of the extensive use of computer-generated imagery in creating the cars and urban landscapes that contribute so much to the production's atmosphere.

A far more significant project was *The Little Mermaid* (1989). John Musker and Ron Clements were slated to direct this movie, and in an advanced stage of preproduction Jeffrey Katzenberg asked them to meet with Howard Ashman, the lyricist of the hit musical *Little Shop of Horrors*, who, with his songwriting partner, Alan Menken, had been called in by Peter Schneider to write one of the numbers for *Oliver & Company.*

"We didn't know much about Howard," says Clements, "except that we liked *Little Shop.* Our first contact with him, I think, was a memo about Sebastian. Sebastian is a crab,

and perhaps a little pompous. . . . Howard's memo said 'How about making Sebastian a Rastafarian?'"

At first, the idea seemed mildly preposterous, but in practice it made a great deal of sense because it gave the character a novel personality, and it permitted Ashman and Menken to introduce a couple of lively West Indian numbers into the score. Musker and Clements were completely won over.

"He knew the Disney movies," says Musker, "and he had an encyclopedic knowledge of American musicals. What's more, he showed us how what works for the musical can be made to work for the animated film. Walt understood that, of course – look at *Snow White* – but it was Howard more than anyone who taught it to our generation."

The conceptual painting, above, by Rowland B. Williams was one of many inspirational works produced to help establish the mood of *The Little Mermaid.* A background painting, left, by Donald Towns exemplifies the production values that were brought to the film

The outcome of all this was that Ashman became coproducer of the movie, along with Musker, and contributed to the evolution of the film in dozens of ways. The familiar Hans Christian Andersen story of the mermaid who falls in love with a human was permitted to retain its period setting, so far as the love story was concerned, but was given many contemporary twists when it came to the underwater scenes. Ariel, the heroine, was presented as a spunky teenager, and Ursula, the villain of the piece, with a voice provided by Pat Carroll, proved to be a splendidly camp character who might have been plucked from some piano bar in the West Village. Andersen's tough ending was exchanged for a happy one, but given the conventions of the Disney animated film – or of the American musical for that matter – this was acceptable.

The Little Mermaid turned out to be, in fact, the most exciting Disney fully animated feature in decades, a turning point comparable in importance with *Roger Rabbit*. Critics and audiences alike fell in love with the heroine and were delighted by Ashman and Menken's lively songs, especially the reggae-tinged "Under

the Sea," which went on to win an Academy Award. And, significantly for the future of Disney animation, these audiences included large numbers of young adults, many of whom went to see the movie more than once. In part this can be explained by the fact the film appeared at a time when the kids who had grown up on a steady diet of television cartoons were becoming wage earners. Unlike earlier generations, they did not give up their affection for animation when they hit puberty. Equally important, though, was the fact that Ashman, Musker, Clements, and the rest of the Disney team were offering something hipper and more sophisticated than had been available in the recent past. It appealed to adults and children alike, and this would be the mark of the Disney animation revival inaugurated by *The Little Mermaid*.

The next movie, however, *The Rescuers Down Under* (1990), was something of a throwback. It was a sequel, of course, to *The Rescuers* and featured once again Miss Bianca and Bernard, the altruistic mice who originated in Margery Sharp's stories. This time the action unfurled mostly in Australia and involved a villainous poacher named Percival McLeach, who is in the business of trapping rare animals and has kidnapped a small boy, Cody, whom he believes can lead him to a giant golden eagle.

The story is adequate, in the style of Disney movies of the sixties and seventies, but the movie's chief interest lies in the fact that it pioneered technical advances that would provide the studio's future films with exceptional production values and much more besides. These advances came with the introduction of the studio's Academy Award–winning CAPS system, a sophisticated computer setup dedicated to the task of managing and enhancing animation material. It is *not* used to generate animation: except for a few special sequences, characters and effects are still drawn by hand, frame by frame. CAPS takes existing animation drawings and effects and backgrounds and combines them so they can be seen in

Two of the architects of Disney's animation revival are Peter Schneider (left), president of feature animation when this photograph was taken and today president of the Walt Disney Studios, and Roy E. Disney, Walt's nephew, who many insiders credit as being the savior of the animation department he has overseen since 1984

The Rescuers Down Under, 1990,
was conceived as a continuation of
the adventures of Miss Bianca and
Bernard. This skillfully made movie,
which takes the altruistic mice to
Australia, has not received the attention it deserves, perhaps because
the story harks back to the middle-
period kind of Disney feature, and the
production as a whole is less rooted
in musical theater than the studio's
more recent successes

video form. It also provides the means to color
images electronically (only backgrounds are
still painted by hand). The CAPS system therefore replaces the old ink and paint department; those department members were
retrained to work at computer workstations,
bringing their years of experience with them.

Enormously expensive, the CAPS system
was fought for by Roy Disney and was justified
economically because it would speed up production and cut costs in the postproduction
phase. At the same time, it allows for far more
complex shots and camera moves, and it can
function as a multiplane camera, permitting
an almost infinite number of levels of action
and background. Most significantly, CAPS
eliminates cels because it generates finished,
high resolution, electronic imagery that can be
transferred directly to film, frame by frame.

As *The Rescuers Down Under* was readied
for its 1990 release date, Disney animation was
poised on the edge of a new and exciting era.

7 A Second Flowering

By the turn of the decade, there were no longer any doubts about the new regime's dedication to the future of feature animation. It was becoming, once more, the core of the entire Disney enterprise. By 1990, the animation department was expanding rapidly and had spread into several buildings scattered around the Glendale industrial park. In addition, at a branch of the feature animation department in Florida, artists worked in full view of visitors to the Disney-MGM Studios®, part of Walt Disney World® Resort near Orlando (see Chapter 10). Far from being just a side-show, this unit has made significant contributions to all productions of the nineties, culminating with *Mulan* (1998), which was produced entirely at the Walt Disney World facility.

The first movie to take full advantage of CAPS and of the enlarged and streamlined department, was a retelling of *Beauty and the Beast,* a film that deserves to stand alongside the best of the early Disney classics. In fact,

Walt Disney had seriously thought about making a film of the story back in the early 1950s, but had abandoned the project. The idea was revived forty years later and almost abandoned again. After a false start, however, the picture was handed over to a team led by executive producer Howard Ashman, producer Don Hahn, directors Gary Trousdale and Kirk Wise, and writer Linda Woolverton. At Ashman's urging, the team emphasized the Beast's story, making him more sympathetic, and strove to make Belle, the heroine, fully three-dimensional. The gloom of the second act was mitigated by making characters such as Cogsworth, Lumiere, and Mrs. Potts – members of the castle's staff transformed into still-life objects – lively instigators of comic relief. Ashman also called for a larger-than-life villain, Gaston, who could be pitted against both Belle and the Beast. Naturally, the film would feature Ashman and Menken songs and a Menken score.

By the time the movie reached theaters, in 1991, the Beast had indeed become more

Beauty and the Beast utilized the talents of young studio artists to produce the most dramatic and satisfying Disney animated film in decades. In Belle it had a particularly strong heroine. She is seen here in a final frame from the movie, above, and in an early concept drawing by Glen Keane, right

Beauty and the Beast

sympathetic (although no less terrifying for that) and Belle had become a strong heroine (if not entirely three-dimensional). Gaston's villainy was skillfully handled; he seems merely a boorish bully in the early going and turns truly evil only toward the climax. The comic relief was handled with great panache, and the songs contributed to both mood and narrative flow. The art direction, layout work, and background paintings all harked back to the standards of the classic era, and, thanks to the magic of the CAPS system, production values were first rate in every respect.

Critics greeted the movie warmly and audiences made it a huge popular success, so much so that it broke all previous box-office records for an animated feature. Even more significantly, perhaps, *Beauty and the Beast* was nominated for an Academy Award in the best picture category – the first time an animated picture was accorded this honor.

Beauty and the Beast, 1991, proved to be a difficult subject to bring to the screen and much preliminary art was produced to help establish plot, mood, and characters. The concept drawing of the Beast carrying Belle through the snow, top, was made by Glen Keane, who would be the principal animator of the Beast. An early version of the story, center, called for a somewhat naturalistic approach and Andreas Deja drew a Gaston who was far more foppish than he later became. The panoramic study, below, was used to help visualize an opening sequence for *Beauty and the Beast* but was eventually abandoned

The Beast's castle

Howard Ashman's story influence led to the Beast's plight becoming pivotal to the story, which is not the case with earlier tellings. It was Ashman too who insisted on characters like Cogsworth, Lumiere, and Mrs. Potts being assigned major roles in order to prevent total gloom from setting in. Lively musical numbers featuring the castle's enchanted objects were introduced into the continuity to provide relief from the somberness of the central theme

Aladdin combined humor with visual stylization to provide fast-moving entertainment. Both qualities were embodied by the Genie, above, and Jafar, left, seen manipulating the befuddled Sultan

Concept art for *Aladdin* by Richard Vander Wende

Aladdin

The studio's next animated feature, *Aladdin*, would prove to be an even greater hit. Except for its element of commercial success, however, *Aladdin* and *Beauty and the Beast* have very little in common. Whereas the impact of *Beauty and the Beast* is due to its ability to plumb emotional highs and lows, the strength of *Aladdin* lies in its witty invention, stylization, and surface flash.

This movie developed as the third directorial outing of John Musker and Ron Clements, who also produced and were the supervising writers. Howard Ashman and Alan Menken were involved once more and wrote six songs for the film (three were used) before Ashman, who had been ill for some time, succumbed to AIDS. After his death, Tim Rice – who was the lyricist of the Broadway muscial *Evita* – was brought in to write the remaining songs with Menken.

Much of the look of *Aladdin* can be attributed to the arrival at the studio of Eric Goldberg, at that time best known for his witty animated commercials. Goldberg's principal animating assignment was the Genie, but his influence can be felt throughout the movie in its graphic look influenced both by Islamic calligraphy and by Goldberg's hero the caricaturist Al Hirschfeld, master of the whiplash line. The Arabian Nights atmosphere also drew on the more than 1,800 photographs taken by layout supervisor Rasoul Azadani in his hometown, Esfahàn, Iran.

Aside from the Genie, the strongest character in the movie is Jafar, the evil vizier animated principally by Andreas Deja. With his broad shoulders, elastic mouth, haughty eyebrows, and expressive hieroglyph of a beard, Jafar is an invitation to unbridled linear invention, and Deja made the most of it.

The character of Aladdin, however, is disappointing, perhaps because the directors tried

Few animated films have ever explored the grotesque for its own sake as thoroughly as *Aladdin*. These drawings by Richard VanderWende are from the film's pre-production phase and give some suggestion of the kind of ideas that were being hatched

105

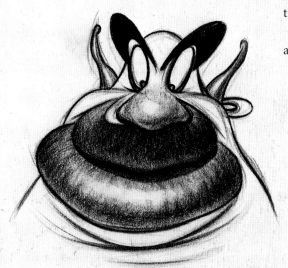

Strong in terms of character animation and story, stunning in its production values, *The Lion King* has proved to be the most successful animated film of all time. The protagonist is the lion Simba, seen in a character-building moment of decision, above, and in a model sheet drawn by Jean Gillmore, right

ROUGH MODEL SHEET
YOUNG SIMBA
PRODUCTION 0885
"King of the Jungle" 1/13/92

The Lion King

too hard to make him contemporary. The result is that he has the attitude of a suburban mall rat and seems out of step with the rest of the cast. Jasmine, on the other hand, is a feisty heroine and many well-realized secondary characters enliven the film, including Abu, Aladdin's monkey; Rajah, Jasmine's pet tiger; and Iago, Jafar's parrot sidekick.

Aladdin features spectacular backgrounds and astonishing examples of the effects animator's art. In the end, though, what makes the movie unforgettable is the virtuoso collaboration between Robin Williams and Eric Goldberg's animation team in creating the Genie. Williams is, of course, famous for his stream-of-consciousness ad-libs, in which he invades and inhabits a menagerie of characters – famous, infamous, anonymous, and androgynous. In the recording studio, Williams improvised around gags devised by the story artists, adding many touches of his own. Working to this voice track, the animators succeeded brilliantly in capturing Williams's chameleon persona on film.

Aladdin reproduced the enchanted atmosphere of the Arabian Nights, and it did enchanted business for the Walt Disney Company, like its predecessor breaking all box-office records for an animated film and becoming one of the all-time top money-earners among all categories of film.

While *Aladdin* was still in production, another team of artists was preparing *The Lion King*. Tom Schumacher was the original producer, but toward the end of 1991 he was promoted to a new position as head of feature animation development and handed over the reins to Don Hahn, although Schumacher remained with the project as executive producer. Roger Allers, story chief for *Beauty and the Beast*, and Rob Minkoff, a gifted animator and story artist, were chosen to direct.

The Lion King was the first Disney animated feature ever to be based on a completely original story. It was also the first since *Bambi* to present animals in an environment that approximates their true habitat.

The Lion King presents the rites of passage of Simba, who, at the beginning of the film, is a newborn lion cub, heir apparent to the kingdom of the Pride Lands, wisely ruled by his father, Mufasa. When Mufasa is killed, during a spectacular stampede sequence, his evil brother, Scar, convinces Simba that he is responsible for his father's death. While Scar takes over the Pride Lands, aided by his hyena lackeys, Simba goes into exile, where he is befriended by Timon the meerkat and Pumbaa the warthog. Finally, though – urged on by his childhood sweetheart Nala, Rafiki the wise old baboon, and (in a scene that recalls *Hamlet)* Mufasa's ghost – Simba returns to claim his heritage.

Throughout *The Lion King*, the African landscape is used to establish both atmosphere and authenticity, as in this image of Rafiki's tree

Spectacular scenes in *The Lion King*
include a musical number involving
the evil hyenas, top, and a computer-
generated stampede, bottom

Timon the meerkat and Pumbaa
the warthog are *The Lion King's*
outstanding comedy characters

The story has a simple arc to it, yet it provides plenty of opportunity for character development and rich detail. Its main theme of filial piety is backed up, as usual, with strong comic relief. And, like *Beauty and the Beast* and *Aladdin*, *The Lion King* is a visually exciting movie that takes full advantage of the spectacular possibilities offered by the CAPS system, especially in the long opening sequence that shows thousands of animals making their way to Pride Rock.

As is so often the case, the villain comes close to stealing the picture. Wittily animated by Andreas Deja, and benefitting from the sardonic voice inflection provided by Jeremy Irons, Scar is an unforgettable piece of work. The film's backgrounds are outstanding, and

the songs, by Tim Rice and Elton John, move the plot along with authority. (Both *Beauty and the Beast* and *The Lion King* were adapted for the stage and became successful Broadway musicals – *The Lion King* won multiple 1998 Tony Awards, including Best Musical.)

The Lion King was released in 1994 and, amazingly, it outperformed both *Beauty and the Beast* and *Aladdin* at the box office, becoming one of the most successful films of all time. It would prove to be the last animated feature to be overseen by Jeffrey Katzenberg. Ten years after joining the Disney team, Katzenberg left the studio, apparently unhappy at not being appointed president of the Walt Disney Company in the wake of Frank Wells's tragic death in a helicopter crash.

These concept studies by Hans Bacher show how, at the pre-production stage, *Lion King* artists were already thinking about the way that animals are seen in wildlife documentaries, in which the telephoto lens sometimes causes dramatic optical effects

For the award-winning Broadway production of *The Lion King* (1997), director/designer Julie Taymor completely revisualized the story, brilliantly integrating African art with innovative stage techniques to bring Simba's story to life in an entirely new way. Above, Rafiki offers wisdom. In the background are shadows of Taymor's imaginative puppets, including gazelles and a zebra

Julie Taymor's color rendering of gazelles, showing a dancer wearing and guiding the puppet

Because it was built around a real historical event, *Pocahontas* called for considerable historical research. Here, pre-production art evokes the dangers of the Atlantic crossing (effects development art by John Emerson and Chris Jenkins)

Designed by Glen Keane, Pocahontas was a demanding character to animate, needing to be conceived in broad enough strokes to command the screen, yet to be capable of displaying considerable delicacy of emotion

Pocahontas tracks John Smith as he explores her world

Pocahontas

These last three films – *Beauty and the Beast, Aladdin,* and *The Lion King* – mark a high point in the recent history of animation. If the next three were to prove less successful, it was only by comparison with the golden trio. Each of them has much to offer, ad, to the extent that each has failings, these are failings caused by the far-reaching ambitions of the Disney animation department.

By the time *Pocahontas* was released in 1995, the animation department was in the process of moving back to Burbank to take possession of a handsome new building across the street from the main lot. (Appropriately, the new animation building is topped with a giant version of the wizard's hat from *The Sorcerer's Apprentice.*)

Pocahontas is built around a real historical event, although it is one greatly distorted by legend: the relationship between Pocahontas, a young Native American woman, and John Smith, a swashbuckling adventurer who was a member of a 1607 British expedition to Virginia. Directed by Mike Gabriel and Eric Goldberg,

the movie presents a love story with awkwardly expressed New Age overtones set against a politically correct subplot in which the corrupt Old World is shown polluting an Eden-like New World wilderness inhabited by noble hunters and foragers living in harmony with nature.

At a certain level, the movie is rather brave in that more than any other Disney animated feature it makes a major play for the adult audience, even at the expense of the school-age fans who traditionally have made such films economically viable. The problem with this turned out to be that the production's idea of adult values was hopelessly naive. Politically correct and artistically satisfying are two very different things. The real-life relationship between Pocahontas and John Smith (actually, the real Pocahontas married another man, John Rolfe, not John Smith) must have been rich in irony. The on-screen version is a soap opera-ish mishmash made up of conventional multicultural clichés.

Still, *Pocahantas* has fine things to offer. Conceived and animated largely by Glen

Pocahontas is notable for historically accurate settings, as can be judged from this concept painting of a Native American longhouse by Justin Brandstater

A street in Medieval Paris, pre-production art by Dave Goetz and Lisa Keene

As is the case in the Victor Hugo novel on which it is based, much of the power of *The Hunchback of Notre Dame* derives from its strong sense of place and its use of architecture as a way of symbolically describing different aspects of the human condition. The pre-production painting by Lisa Keene, above, was based on a drawing by Darek Gogol

Quasimodo rejoices high above Paris

Keane, the heroine has a striking presence and, as producer James Pentecost has noted, the landscape itself plays a key role in the story. "When it's seen from the point of view of the Europeans," says Pentecost, "it's a mysterious new world – both wonderful and scary. . . . Seen from the point of view of the Indians, it's a completely different place in which the trees and animals are not only familiar but have assigned powers within the mythology by which the tribe lives."

By any normal standards, *Pocahontas* was a success at the box office. In comparison with its predecessors, however, its earnings were modest. This disappointing comparison held for the next animated feature as well, *The Hunchback of Notre Dame* (1996).

Like *Pocahontas*, *Hunchback* tried to attract adult audiences, and once again the experiment did not quite succeed. Not that the same mistakes were made. The Disney version of the Victor Hugo story differs in several significant respects from the original, but it maintains much of the novel's complexity, setting up a situation in which psychological richness could have been developed. In fact, the directors – Gary Trousdale and Kirk Wise once again – and the animators came very close to pulling off a remarkable tour de force. Quasimodo's longing to escape into the everyday world is skillfully established, Esmeralda is invested

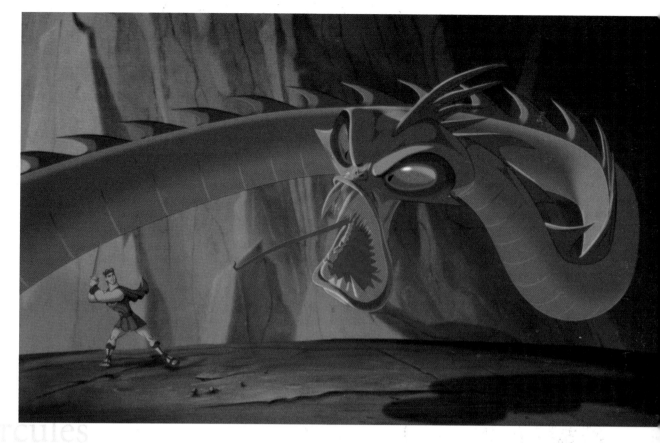

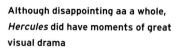

Although disappointing aa a whole, *Hercules* did have moments of great visual drama

with a sensuality new to the Disney canon, and Frollo, the villain of the piece, is presented as a man tormented by conflicting passions rather than as an embodiment of pure evil.

In addition, production values are splendid. The movie incorporates some of the best art direction, layout planning, and background painting found in any animated feature. The city of Paris comes to life in this film, and it teems with raw humanity. Unfortunately, though, the character animation is quite weak in places. Nobody seems to have been able to settle on Quasimodo's size. In some shots he is as tall as Esmeralda, in others he looks like one of the seven dwarfs. Perhaps if the production crew had been given more time to complete this movie, flaws like this would not have slipped by. What could not have been avoided, however, is the problem of Quasimodo himself.

For the most part, adults had no problem with "Quasi." Some children, on the other hand, were frightened by him, and that made him difficult to sell as a sympathetic hero. In short, an important segment of the audience for animated features was turned off by the subject matter, and very little palliative material

was offered. The talking gargoyles, for example, did not appeal much to the average seven-year-old. At the same time, the movie is not sufficiently uncompromising in its presentation of the horrors of medieval class warfare to fully capture the imagination of young adults. A potential masterpiece, *The Hunchback of Notre Dame* ended up by falling between two stools.

It was less disappointing, however, than *Hercules* (1997), a comic-strip romp through the myths of ancient Greece directed by John Musker and Ron Clements. It can be assumed that the studio was hoping for another *Aladdin*, a frothy entertainment enlivened by knowing anachronisms. But, as with *The Hunchback of Notre Dame*, there seems to have been a problem in identifying the audience. It is aimed to be an out-and-out comedy, but the gags are mostly above the heads of children and not sharp enough for adult audiences. In short, the film is sophomoric. The idea of a Motown-style girl group filling in for the traditional Greek chorus is about as clever as this movie gets. That is a device that might have worked with the help of songs by Howard Ashman and Alan Menken, but with music by Menken and

Telling the story of a brave young woman in ancient China, its powerful narrative supported by strong art direction, *Mulan* found favor with both critics and audiences. Here, Mulan is seen being comforted by her father, Fa Zhou, in a contemplative moment, above, and engaged in battle, right

Mulan

lyrics by David Zippel, it falls flat. What is missing as a whole, in fact, is Ashman's sure touch
with musical material and his sharp story
sense. More than anyone since Walt Disney, he
understood what makes an animated movie
work. His death was a great artistic loss, and it
is tragic that he is no longer around to combine his creativity with the great pool of talent
available at Disney today.

Happily, the studio's 1998 animated release,
Mulan, is a considerable improvement on its
three predecessors. The story of a young
Chinese woman who poses as a man to fight
in her father's place, this is the first Disney animated feature to be produced chiefly in the
Florida plant. The talent available there is clearly
of a high order, and the level of character animation is noteworthy. The heroine herself is
portrayed with vigor and restraint, a combina-
tion that allows for a new and more complex
kind of Disney heroine, driven by motives
other than the need for self-assertion or the
search for the man of her dreams.

Mulan has captured the imagination of
audiences of all ages because it is a straightforward story told in a straightforward way. The
production team has resisted the temptation to
sugarcoat the saga of this brave young woman.
As a consequence, the animated adventures of
Mulan retain the universal appeal that have
made this story a classic of Chinese literature
for hundreds of years.

**A pre-production painting for *Mulan*
by Sai Ping Lok, based on layout art
by Gay Lawrence and Valerio Ventura**

117

The first Disney animated feature set in the jungle since *The Jungle Book*, *Tarzan* revealed how much the scope of animation had expanded in the intervening thirty-odd years. In *Tarzan*, animator Glen Keane designed a character with amazing physical attributes, reflecting both his human physiognomy and his upbringing by gorillas. The story had been the inspiration for many live-action films, but only in animation could the hero's awesome prowess be fully realized

Tarzan

Mulan's successor, *Tarzan* (1999), gives a Disney spin to one of the twentieth century's most durable folk heroes, already brought to the screen in almost fifty live-action films but never before touched by the magic of animation. Another 1999 release is *Fantasia 2000*, produced under the supervision of Roy Disney, Jr., a film that combines episodes from the original *Fantasia* with new scenes that explore the technical possibilities open to animators today.

Apart from the products of the feature animation department, there have been other Disney full-length animated films in the past few years. It should be noted, for example, that the television animation department has been responsible for two theatrical releases – *Duck Tales: The Movie* (1990), a mediocre spin-off of a television series, and *A Goofy Movie* (1995), which succeeded very well within its own terms.

Much more important than these, however, and on a par with the best of the conventionally animated movies, was *Toy Story* (1995), in which computer-generated animation was used to create a world realistic enough to sustain a feature-length story. As early as *Midnight in a Toy Shop* (1930), Disney animators had used the familiar notion of toys coming to life as the basis for a cartoon. *Toy Story* did the same thing on a grand scale, telling the story of how Woody the cowboy (with the voice of Tom Hanks) finds his leadership role in the playroom challenged by a newcomer, the pompous astronaut Buzz Lightyear (Tim Allen).

The movie was the result of a collaboration between Disney and Pixar, a computer animation company founded by George Lucas and now owned by Apple computer cofounder Steve Jobs. Directed by John Lasseter, the film was made by placing the latest electronic equipment at the disposal of skilled animators. Assisted by well-conceived art direction, the cyber-assisted animators were able to achieve a remarkable degree of realism. Best of all, this was put to the service of telling a well thought-out story further enhanced by the voice talents of Hanks, Allen, Annie Potts, Don Rickles, Wallace Shawn, and Jim Varney, among others.

Toy Story not only introduced a new era in animation, it did so with such authority that it established itself as an instant classic. Another Disney/Pixar film was immediately put into production and the result was the delightful and visually inventive *A Bug's Life* (1998), featuring the voices of Kevin Spacey, Julia Louis-Dreyfus, and the late Roddy McDowell.

119

For *Toy Story*, Disney teamed up with the digital animation company Pixar to produce the first feature made entirely with computer-generated 3-D animation: a new, high-tech variant on the old theme of toys that come to life when their human owners are not looking. Leading a cast of resourceful toys were the cowboy Woody and the astronaut Buzz Lightyear. Much of the concept art for the movie, left, was created the old fashioned way, using ink, paint, and paper

Toy Story

Toy Story demonstrated conclusively that computer-generated animation had come of age. It showed that successful computer animation depended on some very traditional values - strong character development and story lines. *Toy Story 2* (1999) took the steadfast band of heroes introduced in *Toy Story* and sent them on a new adventure

Like *Toy Story*, *A Bug's Life* gave the Pixar crew the opportunity to play marvelous tricks with scale, since its heroes were even smaller than toys. Above, the intrepid ant Flik arrives in "the city," where Times Square-like billboards are actually stacked food cartons. Comic relief comes in traditional vaudeville packages: a fat caterpillar named Heimlich and a skinny walking stick named Slim, right

A Bug's Life

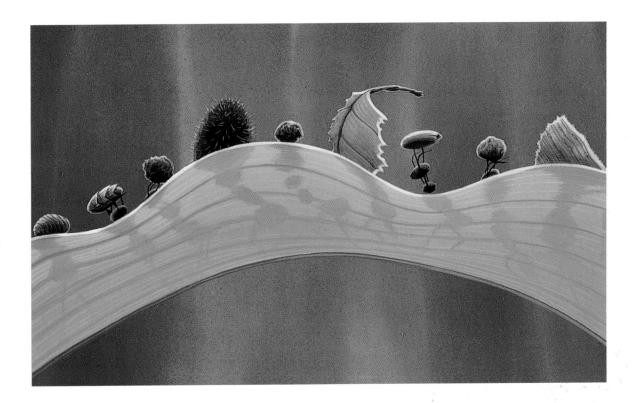

In creating the world of *A Bug's Life*, the Pixar artists made brilliant imaginative use of the computer's ability to replicate natural forms such as leaves and petals

"The Steadfast Tin Soldier," directed by Hendel Butoy and set to music by Shostakovich, combines traditional animation with computer-generated imagery

Spearheaded by Roy E. Disney, *Fantasia 2000* is ushering in the new millennium. A new generation of animators is visually interpreting classical compositions by Beethoven, Shostakovich, Respighi, Saint-Saëns, Elgar, and Stravinsky, performed this time by James Levine and the Chicago Symphony Orchestra. *Fantasia* had originally been conceived as a "repertoire program" that would have changing musical selections. This was not to be, but the new film does honor this ambition by combining six new selections with three favorites from the 1940 classic. Once again, *Fantasia* is being used as a seedbed for new creative concepts and technological innovations in animation

For a selection from Beethoven's "Fifth Symphony," director Pixote Hunt envisioned two shapes dancing on water

Fantasia 2000

Paul and Gaëtan Brizzi directed a nature idyll of beauty and power, set to Stravinsky's "The Firebird Suite"

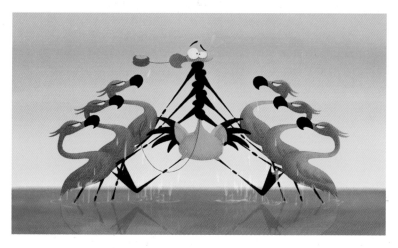

Flamboyant flamingos cavort in a sequence set to Saint-Saëns' "Carnival of the Animals" and directed by Eric Goldberg

Whales leap joyously out of the sea in a scene from another contribution by director Hendel Butoy, with music from Respighi's "Pines of Rome"

Elgar's "Pomp and Circumstance" provides the musical backdrop for Donald Duck and Daisy's adventure when they sail with Noah and his ark, in a selection directed by Francis Glebas

8 Muskets and Mouseketeers

Since Michael Eisner took control of the Walt
Disney Company, it has become a major player
in the live-action film world, and its television
commitments have expanded to the point
where it now owns ABC (American Broadcasting Company), one of the three major networks. It should not be forgotten, however,
that Walt Disney himself was a not inconsider-
able producer of live-action films, and was a
major contributor to the evolution of network
television programming.

Although the "Alice Comedies" had
included live-action material, *The Reluctant
Dragon*, released in 1941, was a major departure
for the studio in that although it incorporated
animated material, it was basically a full-length
live-action film. Fascinating, if somewhat fic-
tionalized, *The Reluctant Dragon* is a guided
tour of the Disney lot during its Golden Age, in
which comic writer and actor Robert Benchley
tries to sell Walt Disney a cartoon idea.

A little later, segments of live-action footage found their way into package films such as
Saludos Amigos. The real breakthrough,
though, came with *Song of the South* (1946),
in which a full complement of professional
actors is used to tell an entirely fictional story.
Cartoon inserts helped sell the movie to the
public, but its success depended on crisp
direction by Harve Foster and strong acting,
notably by James Baskett as Uncle Remus.

Two years later, the studio released *So
Dear to My Heart*, another costume drama
with animated glosses. History then conspired
to push Disney toward a series of all live-
action historical pictures. Because of postwar
monetary restrictions, a significant portion of
Disney financial assets was frozen in Great
Britain. He had access to the money only if it
was being employed there, and on the advice
of his brother Roy, Walt decided to use it to
make films in the British Isles. The fruits of
this venture – *Treasure Island, The Story of
Robin Hood and his Merrie Men, The Sword
and the Rose,* and *Rob Roy, the Highland Rogue*
– were released between 1950 and 1954.

Although it includes fine segments of animation, *Song of the South*, 1946, is primarily a live-action film highlighted by James Baskett's outstanding portrayal of Uncle Remus

These are well-told, satisfying adventure stories full of muskets and longbows and appropriate period detail. *Treasure Island* in particular is a minor masterpiece of the genre, a faithful rendition of Robert Louis Stevenson's classic novel heightened by Robert Newton's mesmerizing performance as Long John Silver. The British historical movies did a good deal to restore the studio's fortunes and to suggest how live-action might feature in Disney's future plans.

At some point soon after World War II, Walt Disney began to think about making a film dealing with America's last frontier: Alaska. Instead of hiring a writer to script an epic, he contacted Al and Elma Milotte, who ran a camera store in Alaska. The Milottes were nature buffs and had some experience with 16mm photography. Disney asked them to film glimpses of Alaskan life that might suggest ideas. As things turned out, the footage of seals that the Milottes shot on the Pribilof Islands turned into the featurette *Seal Island*, which

practically invented the modern nature film, won an Academy Award, and attracted a surprisingly enthusiastic audience of moviegoers.

This film launched the "True-Life Adventures" series, which included feature-length movies such as *The Living Desert*, *The Vanishing Prairie*, *The African Lion*, and *White Wilderness*. Later spin-offs from the True-Life Adventures included the "People and Places" documentary series, and more significantly, the many Disney films – such as *Nikki, Wild Dog of the North* and *The Legend of Lobo* – that blended documentary and staged footage to tell a story.

As far back as the 1930s, Walt Disney had been aware of the potential importance of television – Mickey Mouse cartoons were used in early tests of transmitting equipment – and Disney was careful to retain the television rights to all of his films. In the late 1940s, when other studios were trying to make quick money by selling the home-screen rights to their film libraries, Disney resisted the temptation. This meant that in later years the studio could benefit from theatrical re-releases of classics like *Snow White* and *Fantasia*, while lesser features and shorts could be recycled as part of Disney television shows.

Walt Disney's first experience with TV came in 1950 and 1951 when he produced Christmas specials. Finally, in 1954, he agreed to develop a series for ABC, a decision that had a good deal to do with the fact that ABC was prepared, in return, to make a sizable investment in Disney's proposed theme park. Appropriately, the new series was titled *Disneyland*. Originally broadcast on Wednesday nights, the family-oriented Disney show would survive – under various names and on each of the three major networks – for twenty-nine seasons. Its greatest success came early on, though, when the three episodes of *Davy Crockett* took the country

127

Starring Robert Newton and Bobby Driscoll, *Treasure Island*, 1950, was the first of a series of costume dramas filmed in the British Isles

Buddy Ebsen (left) and Fess Parker starred in *Davy Crockett*, Disney's first television hit

by storm, launching a hit song and an international craze for coonskin hats.

Another hugely popular Disney television program, *The Mickey Mouse Club*, was launched on ABC in 1955 and ran every weekday afternoon until 1959. The show featured the talents of young performers who soon captured the imagination of America's children. The biggest star it produced was Annette Funicello, who went on to have a successful career in films outside the Disney orbit, although still under the guidance of Walt Disney.

In 1954, the year in which the *Disneyland* series was launched, the studio released *20,000 Leagues Under the Sea*, easily its most ambitious live-action film to that point – a big-budget movie with major Hollywood stars (Kirk Douglas, James Mason, Paul Lukas, and Peter Lorre) and state-of-the-art special effects.

Adapted from the Jules Verne novel about Captain Nemo, an idealistic but demented submariner, this project demanded elaborate sets and a great deal of trick photography. Much of the action was shot in a large water tank on one of the Disney soundstages, and location work was done in Jamaica and off Sa

20,000 Leagues Under the Sea, 1954, was a big-budget adventure film with an all-star cast that included James Mason, right, Kirk Douglas, Peter Lorre, and Paul Lukas

The Mickey Mouse Club featured the Mouseketeers, a group of children with no previous show-business experience. Although no one performer was designated as the show's star, Annette Funicello emerged as a great audience favorite and went on to a career in movies

Diego. A highlight of the action is a violent struggle between the crew of the *Nautilus* and a studio-built giant squid. Ultimately, though, *20,000 Leagues Under the Sea* grips our imagination because it is convincing as a battle of ideas and emotions.

Released in 1960, *Swiss Family Robinson* was another big-budget movie from a classic adventure story. With John Mills in the lead role, the film shows how a shipwrecked family learns to cope on a desert island. The production offers some excellent scenic photography, but in the end, the movie lacks the dramatic tension of the best Disney dramas.

The Shaggy Dog, released in 1959, was the first of the studio's zany comedies. Starring Fred MacMurray, who had been seen in many of the screwball comedies of the thirties and early forties, it was in some ways an update of that kind of movie. It was followed by other vehicles tailored to MacMurray's talents, notably *The Absent-Minded Professor* (1961) and *Son of Flubber* (1963). The young British actress Hayley Mills also starred in several Disney films during this period, including costume pieces such as *Pollyanna* and contemporary comedies like *The Parent Trap*.

Between *The Reluctant Dragon* and Walt Disney's death, the studio released more than fifty theatrical live-action feature films, and many more made-for-television movies as well. The most successful of these was *Mary Poppins* (1964). Adapted from P. L. Travers's children's stories, the movie provided Julie Andrews with a spectacular screen debut and smashed box-office records at home and abroad.

Walt Disney had made several attempts to obtain the rights to the Poppins stories, probably intending to adapt them for an animated feature. Finally, he visited the author in London and she agreed to his terms. Back in Burbank, Bill Walsh – a key and underappreciated figure in the evolution of the studio's live-action program – began work on a script with Don DaGradi. (Walsh, the man behind many of Disney's zany comedies, would also coproduce.) The brothers Richard M. and Robert B. Sherman were called in to write music and lyrics.

When it came to casting the magical nanny, Mary Martin and Bette Davis were considered frontrunners, but Disney had seen Julie Andrews on stage in *Camelot* and was very taken with her – especially, so he said, with her whistling ability. She made the char-

Released in 1964, *Mary Poppins* combined live action with interludes of animation - as in this scene with Dick Van Dyke dancing with penguins - and became the biggest commercial success that the Studio would enjoy during Walt Disney's lifetime

acter of Mary Poppins more glamorous than the one we meet on the printed page, and she brought her own charm and spark to the role, in addition to her beautiful singing voice. Walsh and DaGradi transformed fragments from Travers's stories into a continuous narrative marked by a robustness that was strictly their own contribution, and Ms. Andrews fit perfectly into this conception. The film, then, was far from being an exact interpretation of Travers's intentions, but it has its own considerable merits. The story is strong, the comedy is well handled, the musical numbers are outstanding, and the use of animation in key sequences gives the production the unique Disney touch. Throughout the film, the real and imaginary are combined in inventive and believable ways. In short, all of the studio's resources were pooled to produce a motion picture that probably could not have been made with such panache anywhere else.

The greatest of these resources, Walt Disney himself, would soon be gone. For a while, though, the studio continued to make the kind of live-action family films he had espoused.

Walt Disney picked Julie Andrews to play Mary Poppins in part because he was impressed by her whistling ability

The Love Bug (1969) – developed, written, and produced by Bill Walsh – inaugurated a successful series of films about Herbie, a Volkswagen with a mind of its own. *Bedknobs and Broomsticks* (1971) was a lively fantasy adventure featuring Angela Lansbury, and *Freaky Friday* (1976) was the best of a number of Disney films starring Jodie Foster.

The video-game fantasy *Tron* (1982) made spectacular use of computer-generated imagery, but was a disappointment at the box office. *Tron* was one of the films made during the brief tenure of Tom Wilhite – former head of the Disney publicity department – as vice president of creative development. Along with *Tron*, Wilhite was largely responsible for a number of interesting movies geared toward the young adult audience (a potentially more profitable demographic market), but the Disney name kept these older audiences away.

With this in mind, Ron Miller, head of production, decided in the early eighties to begin issuing a new and more adult-oriented line of films for which a different brand name – Touchstone – was eventually adopted. With Wilhite in charge of the program, Touchstone made its debut with a major hit in the form of *Splash* (1984), starring Tom Hanks and Darryl Hannah and directed by Ron Howard. It quickly became apparent that Touchstone was a good idea, but it came too late to prevent the studio from being plunged into a state of turmoil later that year. Touchstone would come fully into its own only after the team led by Michael Eisner, Frank Wells, and Roy Disney had taken the helm.

It would take several chapters to adequately discuss the live-action movies that have been released by the studio since 1984. These range from the series of low comedies built around Jim Varney's Ernest P. Worrell character to films for the art-house market released by highly independent Disney subsidiaries such as Miramax. Among the films released by Disney's in-house divisions – Touchstone, Hollywood Pictures, and Walt Disney – have

David Warner was one of the stars of *Tron*, 1982, which made use of electronic effects to place human protagonists inside a video game. Among the pioneering filmmakers on *Tron* was John Lasseter, who went on to be a creative force behind Pixar

Splash!, 1984, starring Tom Hanks and Darryl Hannah, was the first Disney feature to be aimed at a sophisticated adult audience

Bette Midler appears in *Ruthless People*, 1986

been many hits such as Paul Mazursky's *Down and Out in Beverly Hills* (1986) and other Bette Midler showcases, including *Ruthless People* (1986), *Outrageous Fortune* (1987), *Beaches* (1989), and *Scenes from a Mall* (1991). Barry Levinson directed a couple of excellent comedies, *Tin Men* (1987) and *Good Morning, Vietnam* (1988). The latter starred Robin Williams, who also took the lead in the ambitious and subtly subversive *Dead Poets Society* (1989).

Other important movies of the period were *The Color of Money*, Martin Scorsese's 1986 sequel to *The Hustler*, *New York Stories* (1989), and *Pretty Woman* (1990). A huge commercial success, the last film was a far cry from traditional Disney fare, starring Julia Roberts as a prostitute who redeems and is redeemed by a yuppie overachiever played by Richard Gere. That same year saw the release of *Dick Tracy*, directed by and starring Warren Beatty.

These were all Touchstone movies. The Walt Disney label was used for family-oriented pictures like *Honey, I Shrunk the Kids* (1989) and its 1992 sequel *Honey, I Blew Up the Kid*.

Robin Williams gave one of his most affecting performances in *Dead Poets Society*, 1989

133

A variation on the Pygmalion theme in which the heroine is a Hollywood hooker rather than a cockney flower girl, *Pretty Woman* was one of the major hits of 1990. Here, Richard Gere takes Julia Roberts shopping on Rodeo Drive

Released in 1990, *Dick Tracy* was an imaginative exploration of pop culture directed by Warren Beatty, who also starred

Sister Act, 1992, was an enormously successful vehicle for Whoopi Goldberg

Honey, I Shrunk the Kids, 1989, was a successful return to the kind of special-effects comedy the Studio had exploited effectively in the sixties and seventies

Hollywood Pictures, meanwhile, was snaring the teenage audience with offerings such as *Arachnophobia* (1990), *The Hand that Rocks the Cradle* (1992), and *Encino Man* (1992).

Films with a broader appeal have included *Sister Act* (1992) and *Sister Act 2: Back in the Habit* (1994), popular hits for Whoopi Goldberg. Another commercial success was *Father of the Bride* (1991), with Steve Martin and Diane Keaton, while *The Mighty Ducks* (1994) not only launched a series of movies but also led to the acquisition, by the Walt Disney Company, of a National Hockey League franchise.

Tim Burton, who had begun his career as a Disney animator, returned to the studio to produce *The Nightmare Before Christmas*, a 1993 feature made with stop-action animation, and later directed *Ed Wood*, an affectionate portrait of the man who made some of the worst movies in the history of Hollywood.

While this remarkable slate of live-action movies was being put together, Disney was plunging deeper and deeper into television. The company had entered the cable TV world in 1983 with The Disney Channel®, an outlet for family programming. In the second half of the eighties, more and more effort was invested in making Disney a force in television animation, an area it had previously avoided. This led to well-received series like *The Gummi Bears*, *The New Adventures of Winnie the Pooh*, *Duck-Tales*, *TaleSpin*, *Goof Troop*, and *Gargoyles*.

Disney also became involved in the situation comedy market, generally by entering into coproduction partnerships, which led to series such as *The Golden Girls*, *Blossom*, *Dinosaurs*, and the enormously popular *Home Improvement*.

Finally, in 1996, the Walt Disney Company acquired ownership of a major television network – the American Broadcasting Company and its various subsidiaries. Appropriately, perhaps, it was ABC that had given Walt Disney his first weekly TV series and had helped finance the Disneyland theme park. The acquisition of the network had the effect of making Disney one of the great media conglomerates – a communications giant far removed from the storefront studio that had begun operations in Hollywood almost three-quarters of a century earlier.

137

Armageddon, 1998, was Disney's entry into the disaster movie field, but not a reach for the studio that had produced *20,000 Leagues Under the Sea* more than forty years before. An intrepid gang of oil drillers led by Bruce Willis blast off into space to save Earth from a rogue asteroid

Tim Burton's *The Nightmare Before Christmas*, 1993, added a stop-motion animation feature to the Disney repertoire

9 Beyond Film

Walt Disney was a man with a knack of doing the right thing at the right time – a person with an almost uncanny instinct for gauging what the public wanted and with the courage to act on his intuitions. Never was this more evident than in the most important of his postwar endeavors.

Disneyland Park grew from a seed that had been germinating in Disney's mind for fifteen or twenty years, since the time when he had taken his daughters to local amusement parks and longed for something more. It was only in the early 1950s, however, that economic conditions provided him with the opportunity to pursue his dream. By then he had become very involved with trains as a hobby, building himself a backyard railroad and toying with the idea of running a full-size narrow-gauge railway around the Burbank studio. This in turn led him to think about amusement parks once again, and specifically about a park encircled by a railroad. At first he investigated the possibility of building such a park across the street from the studio, but the property avail-able was too small for the concept that was evolving in his mind, and he encountered problems with planning permissions.

After this preliminary exploration of the idea, in 1952 Disney set up an organization named WED (his initials) to begin serious work on planning a park for a yet unchosen site. WED was mostly made up of artists co-opted from the animation department. They soon came to be known as "Imagineers" and eventually the unit they worked for was renamed WDI, Walt Disney Imagineering.

As concepts for the park took shape on the drawing board, the organization researched various sites in southern California. Soon Disney was the owner of 160 acres of orange groves in the Orange County community of Anaheim, selected because the soon-to-be-completed Santa Ana Freeway would pass within a few hundred yards of the property, linking it with metropolitan Los Angeles.

It was not easy to sell investors on the idea of Disneyland. Even Walt's brother Roy was skeptical, and bankers were apt to point out that conventional Coney Island–style amusement parks were going out of business all over the country. Disney patiently pointed out that what he had in mind was a different kind of park – a theme park – but he still had to dig deep into his own pockets before eventually finding two large companies prepared to put money into the project. One was the American Broadcasting Company–Paramount Theaters group, which was anxious to have Disney produce a television series for them (see Chapter 8). The other was Western Printing and Lithographing, which had long published Disney books. (Each company made its investment on the understanding that Disney would have the right to buy them out if the park was a success. Needless to say, this right was exercised before too many years had passed.) With this money in place, banks and other financial institutions were prepared to lend the rest.

Now work went ahead at full speed to implement Walt Disney's vision. The plan called for a vintage railroad to define the perimeter of the property, with its main station located at the park entrance. Once inside, the visitor would pass down Main Street – an idealized facsimile of the kind of Midwestern town Walt had known as a boy. At the far end of Main Street would be the Sleeping Beauty Castle, which would serve as the hub of a cluster of themed areas – Adventureland, Frontierland, Fantasyland, and Tomorrowland – through which visitors would circulate. In a sense, each of these zones was conceived as a glorified movie set. In Frontierland, for example, the

Walt Disney stands beside the trolley tracks on Disneyland's Main Street

visitor might imagine himself entering a Hollywood Western, and other "lands" evoked other movie genres, from costume drama to science fiction. Many attractions would draw upon the Disney animated films for inspiration, and the whole park would be knit together by a web of transportation that would range from horse-drawn trolleys to aerial tramways. (The monorail would be installed a little later.)

Some features of Disneyland had been foreshadowed by fairs like St. Louis's Louisiana Purchase Exposition and Chicago's Century of Progress Exposition. What made Disney's park different, however, was the fact that it was "user-friendly" years before that term was coined. Disneyland was built to a human scale and was without the noisily competing attractions commonly encountered in the rival pavilions that make up a world's fair. Disneyland was planned to encourage the visitor to stroll at his own pace and enjoy all the varied attractions at his leisure.

139

This imaginary aerial view of the proposed park, drawn by Herb Ryman, was used as a sales tool when Walt Disney was presenting the idea of Disneyland to potential investors

Disneyland opened on July 17, 1955. Television crews were on hand to record the opening ceremonies, while thirty thousand guests thronged the park. A good deal of journalistic attention was focused on the plaque in Town Square that read as follows:

TO ALL WHO COME TO THIS HAPPY PLACE:

WELCOME.

DISNEYLAND IS YOUR LAND. HERE AGE

RELIVES FOND MEMORIES OF THE PAST . . .

AND HERE YOUTH MAY SAVOR THE CHALLENGE

AND PROMISE OF THE FUTURE.

DISNEYLAND IS DEDICATED

TO THE IDEALS, THE DREAMS, AND THE HARD

FACTS THAT HAVE CREATED AMERICA . . .

WITH THE HOPE THAT IT WILL BE A SOURCE OF

JOY AND INSPIRATION TO ALL THE WORLD

JULY 17, 1955

When those words were written, even Walt Disney could not have dreamed quite how thoroughly his park would capture the imagination of the world, or how it would virtually demand siblings. Before long, however, he was beginning to think about how ideas implicit in Disneyland could be expanded elsewhere. The 1964 New York World's Fair provided opportunities to experiment, and he then turned his attention to Florida. In part, his intention was to build a basic theme park that would become a magnet for the East Coast as Disneyland was a magnet for the West. Also, by acquiring a much larger tract of land, he wanted to avoid the problem of urban sprawl that had been attracted to the perimeter of Disneyland, where he had no control over the surroundings. Finally, he wanted his new Magic Kingdom to be just part of a complex that would include not only new kinds of theme parks and attendant resorts but also a new kind of experimental community, which he dubbed EPCOT (Experimental Prototype Community of Tomorrow).

By October 1965 – ten years after Disneyland opened – Disney had put together a package of Florida land as large as San Francisco. (Astonishing by today's standards, it cost just over $5,000,000.) On November 15 of that same year, the Walt Disney World project was officially launched. Sadly, Walt Disney himself did not live to see even the first phase built, but the last year of his life was devoted largely to making sure that his vision would be carried out.

John Hench, a senior vice president of WDI and dean of the Imagineering team, described Roy Disney's report of one of his last visits to his brother. "Walt was hallucinating, but it was as if he could see this map of his property on the ceiling, and he was pointing to it with one hand and describing it, explaining why we'd have to build an east-west road running through, and so on. It was as if the whole thing was there in full detail. He was obsessed."

This aerial view of The Magic Kingdom at Walt Disney World in Florida shows a Main Street parade in progress.

Cinderella Castle at Walt Disney World

"The problem was," says Marty Sklar, president of WDI, "that when Walt died, many people thought we couldn't carry it through without him."

Luckily Walt had convinced Roy Disney that it was imperative that Walt Disney World be built.

"Personally," he told Hench, "I had my doubts, but I had to do it for Walt – because if I hadn't he would have given me hell when I died."

Roy Disney devoted himself to seeing that the Florida Magic Kingdom was completed just as his brother Walt had wanted it. It opened on schedule in October of 1971. A few weeks later, just five days before Christmas, Roy Disney – who had been looking forward to a well-deserved retirement – was dead, his life shortened, some speculated, by his exertions in realizing his brother's final dream.

Since the deaths of the Disney brothers, expansion in Florida and later into Japan and Europe has enabled Disney's Imagineers to explore many aspects of the theme park concept, from the creative marriage of entertainment and science found at EPCOT Center to the cultural variations on basic Disney themes introduced at Tokyo Disneyland and Disneyland Paris, themes that still find their archetypal expression in the two original Magic Kingdoms, in California and Florida.

John Hench – a key creative figure at WED and WDI for more than forty years – has given extensive thought to the reasons for Walt Disney's success with the parks and in his career as a whole.

142

A horse-drawn streetcar in Town Square at Disneyland

An aerial view of Big Thunder
Mountain at Walt Disney World

"Part of it, I suppose," he says, "was Walt's exploitation of very old survival patterns. . . . We've carried these things around for twenty million years, in our DNA chains or whatever. . . . The things that please us are obviously the ones that boost our survival potential – and the ones we don't like are those that threaten us. . . .

"Mickey was so-called Lollipop Art – because he was made from circles. I'm over-simplifying it, but circles have never hurt any-body – they are women's breasts and clouds and other soft forms. Felix the Cat, on the other hand, was full of angles and sharp points. . . . [The softness] explains the success of Mickey, who just won't quit. Walt was a highly intuitive person and he sensed these things. . . .

"[He] had a high sensitivity, I think, for timing and the way things relate to each other – and this, of course, came from the film work. This is what film is all about, connecting ideas so that they relate to one another. . . . Live-

Mickey Mouse plays host in Mickey's
Toontown

143

action filming has to count on lots of accidents, but in a cartoon we could gradually eliminate the things that contradicted what we wanted to say. With the background we had [in animation], this was a very easy thing to apply to the third dimension."

Hench explains that, in the theme parks, Disney was able to create controlled environments structured, much like animated movies, in such a way as to almost guarantee the visitor a good time: "They're an attempt to relate one idea to the next. You don't have to drop one before you pick up another – they carry through. This again comes from the motion-picture background. The division into related themes gives a sense of continuity."

The motion-picture influence can be felt in almost every one of the Disney theme attractions. Whether it is the Haunted Mansion or Pirates of the Caribbean, each experience is planned in much the same way as a short cartoon, storyboarded first so that its "narrative" can be refined before anything is built. Once the story is established, it is then engineered so

Soon after World War II, Walt Disney tries out a dance routine with Buddy Ebsen. Ebsen's routine was filmed and served as the basis for Disney's first mechanical figure, the ancestor of all the Audio-Animatronics figures in the parks

that some kind of vehicle (usually a car on rails) carries the visitor through the pre-arranged sequence of events. These events are experienced in three dimensions, but otherwise the experience is not unlike that of watching a movie.

In many attractions, Disney's Imagineers have introduced the element of three-dimensional animation through Audio-Animatronics® – figures that can be programmed to perform sometimes complex routines. Long before he built Disneyland, Walt Disney was a collector of clockwork toys. In the mid-forties, he began to experiment with programmed, mechanical puppets, but the machinery then available was too bulky to make this practical. The building of Disneyland prompted a new round of experiments. The first models employed simple cam and lever joints, but soon trials were made with more flexible systems employing pneumatic and hydraulic power transmission controlled by electrical inputs. These were efficient enough to supply the kind of crude movements needed for such figures as the animals dotted around the Jungle Cruise. Next someone came up with the idea of using sound recorded on magnetic tape as a way of activating the pneumatic and hydraulic valves. Sound impulses could be used to trigger mechanisms, buried within lifelike plastic figures, that could control movements down to the flicker of an eyelid. The tape system also permitted these movements to be synchronized with prerecorded dialogue or music.

The first Audio-Animatronics figures built were exotic birds, which eventually formed the basis of Disneyland's Enchanted Tiki Room. In 1964, the new technology was given a far more spectacular outing at the New York World's Fair, where Disney staged "Great Moments with Mr. Lincoln" at the Illinois pavilion. Visitors were confronted with a startlingly life-like facsimile of the nation's sixteenth president. Lincoln not only spoke but emphasized his thoughts with naturalistic gestures. His eyes raked the audience, as though challenging opponents to debate. He shifted his weight

from one foot to another, and his expression changed with the sense of his words. No one had seen anything like this before and the impact was extraordinary.

The success had not been easily won. Indeed, it had seemed that Lincoln might never be finished in time for the fair. The sheer energy pent up in the pneumatic and hydraulic systems of such a figure is considerable, and unless that energy is precisely regulated the figure can become violent. Before he was tamed, Mr. Lincoln smashed his chair and threw mechanical fits that threatened the safety of those near him.

Once this problem had been solved, however, there was nothing to stop the Imagineers from populating the Disney parks with all manner of Audio-Animatronics figures, ranging from the Mickey Mouse Revue to the Hall of Presidents (which features Lincoln surrounded by his peers).

Later, computer chips and other electronic innovations helped make the mechanical figures still more sophisticated, but their success has always been predicated upon the Disney artists' decades of experience with animation. They understand, for example, the importance of animating the eyes because, as in a cartoon, the attention of viewers is automatically drawn to the eyes. A character may express surprise more effectively by widening his eyes or lifting an eyebrow than by throwing up his hands in shock. Without this kind of insight, all the engineering skill that goes into these figures would be wasted.

For all the technological innovations to be found in the Magic Kingdom, the Disney organization's primary expertise is show business. The theme parks are a kind of total theater that provides entertainment for millions of visitors each year.

10 Themes and Variations

In its early days, Walt Disney World consisted of the Magic Kingdom, three hotels, various satellite resort areas, a small model community, three golf courses, and a magnificent 7,500-acre wildlife preserve designed to save the last vestige of the Central Florida wilderness. (This preserve is carefully isolated from developed sections of the resort.)

Already, in this skeletal form, Walt Disney World was a testing ground for enlightened technology, innovative urban planning, and responsible environmental management. The advanced building code encouraged the use of state-of-the-art construction techniques. The Magic Kingdom itself was built on a giant platform, which permitted a network of corridors, storage areas, and service systems beneath the principal areas of the park. This infrastructure allowed supplies and costumed employees to be delivered at any point in the park without ever being seen on the streets. Garbage could be disposed of without benefit of conspicuous trucks.

Building Walt Disney World was rather like creating a medium-size city from scratch. There was nothing there but swamp, and everything had to be brought in from somewhere else. Nor was there any trained workforce on hand. To staff the park and the hotels, people had to be hired from all over the country and trained. Despite some early glitches, however, the first phase of Walt Disney World was soon running smoothly, and Imagineers were encouraged to turn their attention toward EPCOT, which had been Walt Disney's main reason for developing the Florida property.

Disney envisioned EPCOT as an actual community. When he announced the project, in 1966, he described his aims in the following terms:

"I don't believe there's a challenge anywhere in the world that's more important to people everywhere than finding solutions to the problems of our cities. But where do we begin . . . how do we start to answer the great challenge?

The focal point of EPCOT Center, comparable to the castles in the Magic Kingdoms, is Spaceship Earth, a geodesic sphere housing a theme show devoted to the history of communications.

When EPCOT Center was being planned, a flexible master model enabled Disney's Imagineers to experiment with many arrangements of the various elements

"Well, we're convinced we must start with the public need. And that need is not just for curing the ills of the old cities.... EPCOT is . . . an experimental prototype community that will always be in a state of becoming. It will never cease to be a living blueprint of the future. . . .

"We don't presume to know all the answers. In fact we're counting on the cooperation of American industry to provide their best thinking during the planning of our . . . community. And most important of all, when EPCOT has become a reality, and we find the need for technologies that don't even exist today, it's our hope that EPCOT will stimulate American industry to develop new solutions that will meet the needs of people expressed right here in this experimental community."

147

The participation of industry was an important part of Disney's idea. "It seems clear in retrospect," says Marty Sklar, "that Walt used the 1964 New York World's Fair as a stepping-stone toward EPCOT. Certainly we didn't need the extra work at the time, but it gave Walt access to the chief executives of GE and other companies he would want to deal with in the future."

The first designs for EPCOT show a domed city that has its roots both in the work of visionary planners like R. Buckminster Fuller and in pop culture versions of the future that might be found in a Buck Rogers comic strip.

"Had Walt Disney lived," Michael Eisner speculates, "I'm sure that EPCOT would have evolved, just like everything else he worked on.... What he left behind . . . is just the first expression of an idea he didn't have time to follow through on."

This is probably true, and certainly the single issue of setting up a government for such a city might have presented insurmountable legal difficulties. (How do you guarantee democratic rights in a place that of necessity functions under corporate control?) Still, there is something about the vision of an experimental community that is a perfect expression of the belief in progress that was so characteristic of Americans of Walt Disney's generation.

For Disney, the distance from Main Street to EPCOT was not so very great.

After Walt Disney's death, it was not until the mid-seventies that EPCOT came under serious consideration. Its champion now was Disney's protegé Card Walker, who had become president of Walt Disney Productions. Walker understood that the original EPCOT idea would be difficult to sell to the financial community. The Imagineers were therefore asked to rethink the basic idea in the form of a theme park that would be "a showcase for prototype concepts" and "an ongoing forum of the future."

This new version of EPCOT would be something like a permanent world's fair, with one group of pavilions representing man's technological challenge (Future World) and another presenting the cultures of various nations (World Showcase). It would differ from a world's fair, however, in that the pavilions would be built to complement one another rather than compete for attention. It would be pleasingly organized around circular ponds and a large central lagoon.

The multinational aspect of the project

The World Showcase section of EPCOT utilizes expertise derived from filmmaking to evoke different countries and cities, such as Venice and Paris. In the case of Paris, the Eiffel Tower is built as a large miniature projecting above the mansard roofs, just as it might be for a movie set. The illusion is quite striking, especially at dusk when the surrogate tower becomes a silhouette against the Florida sky

was not entirely new. One of Walt Disney's earliest ideas for Disneyland had been for an international street (it was to branch off from Town Square). Similarly, Future World had its roots in Tomorrowland. At the crossroads between Future World and World Showcase would be an exhibit called the American Adventure, inspired by Herman Melville's observation that "America has been settled by people of all nations. . . . We are not a nation so much as a world."

EPCOT finally opened in October of 1982, eleven years after the opening of Walt Disney World. Visitors could eat shepherd's pie in an English pub or *foie de veau* in a French bistro, then move on to the AT&T pavilion. As had been the case with the Magic Kingdom, early attendance figures were disappointing, but ticket sales built steadily and over time EPCOT Center (as it came to be officially known) developed into a formidable foil for the Magic Kingdom. Over the years it has thrived and expanded – with spectacular new shows, such as The Living Seas, featuring "sea cabs" and an underwater restaurant. The Imagineers, back in California, have stayed

current with new developments in science and technology so that exhibits can be updated as soon as possible, and new ones built when necessary. More even than the other theme parks, EPCOT Center is an environment in a state of perpetual renewal.

Early in 1985, Michael Eisner raised the idea of an arts pavilion for EPCOT Center. This quickly evolved into a concept for a motion-picture arts pavilion, but eventually Eisner and Frank Wells decided that was too modest. What they came up with instead was an entirely new theme park that would at the same time be a working motion-picture studio; where visitors could enjoy movie-oriented rides and exhibits, and at the same time watch a film being made on an actual soundstage and see animators at work on a forthcoming Disney feature.

To maximize the appeal of such a park, it was considered desirable to supplement access to the Disney backlog of films by acquiring rights to another library of classics. The one that was available proved to be the cornucopia of productions turned out over the decades by MGM/UA. As part of the deal to license these

149

films for limited use, an agreement was struck to use the MGM name and trademark in connection with the park.

The Disney-MGM Studio opened to the public in 1989. It featured reconstructions of Grauman's Chinese Theater and Hollywood Boulevard, along with a New York street and special-effects movies conceived and directed by master entertainers George Lucas and Jim Henson. At the heart of the complex were the working soundstages and animation studio. Giving the public access to the latter, without disturbing the artists at work, was something of a challenge.

"We had to meet with animators," says Bob Weis, chief designer for the studio tour, "and try to understand how they work. What kinds of personality quirks do they have? How can you make them feel comfortable when you're about to violate the sanctity of their working environment by bringing guests through to stare over their shoulders?"

The fact that the plan succeeded can be judged by the fact that, as noted in Chapter 7, *Mulan* was produced almost entirely on the Florida lot under conditions of public scrutiny.

The Disney-MGM Studios complex has the advantage of providing an appropriate home for anything connected with the entertainment industry. Teenage Mutant Ninja Turtles have been part of this park, and the Muppets too. The Tower of Terror is a thrill ride that draws on memories of Rod Serling's *Twilight Zone*, and George Lucas has contributed a spectacular Indiana Jones show.

Opened in 1994, the Tower of Terror - located on Sunset Boulevard in the Disney-MGM Studios - has become one of the most popular attractions at Walt Disney World. Its sedate Edwardian architecture and decor belies its raison d'être, a *Twilight Zone* adventure that culminates in a hair-raising ride in a runaway elevator

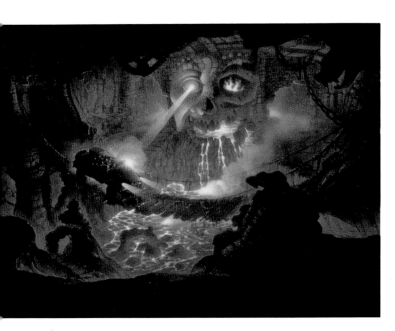

Concept art for the Indiana Jones Adventure

The most recent addition to Walt Disney World is Disney's Animal Kingdom, which opened to the public on Earth Day, April 22, 1998. This 500-acre theme park offers a realistic African safari that permits visitors to see lions, hippos, and other wild animals up close in approximations of their natural settings. In other exhibits, the park celebrates the whole world of animals – real, extinct, and imaginary – and provides live entertainments and thrill rides.

A different kind of Walt Disney World attraction has been The Disney Institute. Located in the Disney Village Resort, here guests participate in programs that, to quote Michael Eisner, "are personally relevant to their lives, from the arts to fitness and health. These programs [are] hands-on and interactive. Guests can help run a radio station, learn circus acts, take cooking classes – even produce their own animated short."

On the edge of Walt Disney World, a new community called Celebration is coming into being. This has been described as "a think tank in the form of a living community." Celebration

is hardly as radical in concept as Walt Disney's original idea for EPCOT, but still it features buildings by leading architects and the opportunity for industry to bring in experimental technologies.

"Walt's original ideas are very much alive," says Marty Sklar. "We never really forgot about them. It was just a question of saving them for the right moment."

It could be argued that Walt Disney, an Everyman of genius, was the prototypical American of his generation, and while he cherished the values and institutions of Middle America, he also seemed to feel, in a very straightforward way, that America's ethnic plurality permitted him to tap into other cultures and environments from around the world. In his movies, he explored British historical legend, European folklore, and the wildlife of several continents. He did not build his proposed International Street at Disneyland, but Africa was present (in the form of the Jungle Cruise), as was the colorful architecture of the Caribbean, half-timbered cottages out of Bavarian forests, and even a simulation of one of Europe's natural marvels, the Matterhorn. EPCOT Center carried the international theme still further and it was only a matter of time before the question of building a Disney theme park abroad would be placed on the agenda.

This New York street is part of the Disney-MGM Studios' back lot

The first move came from Japan.

Dreamland – an unlicensed imitation of Disneyland – was built there in the early sixties but failed, largely because it lacked Disney characters, let alone Disney expertise. In 1978, representatives of Japan's Keisi Electric Railway Company approached Disney with an invitation to build an authentic Disney park on a 201-acre property on the outskirts of Tokyo. Disney management was worried about such factors as Tokyo's cold winters and cultural differences, but they were persuaded that these could be overcome and so, with Japanese financial backing, Tokyo Disneyland was built under Disney supervision, opening on April 15, 1983.

Anyone who has visited Disneyland in Anaheim would find much about its Japanese cousin very familiar – the fairytale castle at the hub, Fantasyland, Adventureland, and Tomorrowland. Frontierland has become Westernland but retains features such as Big Thunder Mountain, the Country Bear Theater, and the Mark Twain Riverboat. But there are significant differences, too. No railway circles the park and, most significantly, perhaps, Main Street has been replaced by a glass-covered arcade

The most recent addition to Walt Disney World is Disney's Animal Kingdom. The park offers a realistic African Safari, right, as well as elements of fantasy drawn from Disney animated features, such as the Tree of Life, above, adapted from *The Lion King*

The town of Celebration, above and right, finally brings to Walt Disney World the living community that Walt envisioned when he was designing EPCOT

known as World Bazaar. In practice, this offers many of Main Street's familiar attractions while also offering protection from inclement weather.

Cultural differences had little impact on the park's design. As the investors had promised, Japanese citizens flocked to Tokyo Disneyland precisely because it was "so American." The total attendance at the Tokyo park for its first ten years was greater than the total population of Japan.

The notion of building a Disney theme park in Europe had been discussed as early as the seventies, but there had been no follow-through at the time because, as with Japan, there had been concerns about climate and cultural differences. The success of the Tokyo park began to change those attitudes and preliminary discussions were held with various governments. It was after the Eisner management team took over, however, that real progress began to be made. Spain and Portugal (blessed with California-like climates) both campaigned actively for the park. In the end, however, it was decided to build EuroDisney –

as it was first called – on the outskirts of Paris. Michael Eisner favored this site because he saw Paris as being the hub of the European continent.

Surprisingly, perhaps, the Paris park faced more cultural challenges than its Tokyo counterpart. Many people in France, and elsewhere in Europe, see Americanization as a threat to homegrown cultures. The design team went out of its way to blunt potential criticism.

"It wasn't like Anaheim or Florida," says Tony Baxter, senior vice president for creative development at WDI. "In France we were going up against fine shopping, historical architecture, and a landscape that defines the words 'charming' and 'pastoral.' We had to go into that environment and redefine Disneyland."

Some decisions, he says, were relatively easy:

"Rethinking the Old West, for example. Walt had visualized it as an idyllic, pastoral Mississippi River landscape . . . the perfect escape for commuters who had been sitting in a traffic jam on the Santa Ana Freeway. But Europeans are looking for something completely different. . . . When they think of the Old West, they think of the *Wild* West. An exciting, energetic place. We realized that our EuroDisney Frontierland would have to reflect that. What we would have to give them was the raucous, roaring atmosphere of the 1849 Gold Rush . . . and we would have to cater to their fascination with Native American culture, and to their Hollywood-nurtured love of the rowdy world of the cowboy, including the rustler and the bad guy."

Far more difficult, Baxter reports, was deciding what to do with the castle. When you're a short drive from the actual castles of the Loire Valley, the competition is tough, and so the Imagineering team decided on a truly "storybook" approach that would not invite direct comparison with the real thing.

The planners also found that, unlike the Japanese, Europeans *were* expecting to find reflections of their own world in the park. The contract with the French government called for appropriate tributes to French civilization and European culture in general.

"One way we tried to do this," explains Baxter, "was to replace Tomorrowland with something called Discoveryland, which was based around the idea of Jules Verne's Discovery Bay. Verne's idea of the future had influenced Walt, yet it remained very European, very French."

Not that Disneyland Paris (as the park has been renamed) is entirely without American touches. Its Main Street is, if anything, even more explicitly American than those in California and Florida. Nearby is a huge entertainment center known as Festival Disney, home to a Wild West show and to streets represent-

The Château at the hub of Disneyland Paris is the ultimate storybook castle

Visitors to the Magic Kingdom at Walt Disney World enjoy the planned scares of Alien Encounter

Sculptural form, dramatic illumination, and the theatrical use of color are made to play crucial roles in the way the theme parks are brought to life. As the evening sky darkens, thousands of lights transform the Orbitron and Space Mountain in Tomorrowland at Walt Disney World, flooding the scene with color that heightens the sense of nocturnal excitement

ing American destinations such as New York, Los Angeles, and Key West, complete with steak houses and country-and-western bars.

When it opened in 1992, Disneyland Paris experienced teething troubles, largely due to overexpenditure on hotels that remained underbooked thanks to the proximity of the park to Paris's great reservoir of tourist accommodations, ranging from the Ritz to modest pensions. Park attendance was good from the first, however, and refinancing involving Prince Alwaleed of Saudi Arabia, chairman of the United Saudi Commercial Bank, helped keep plans for expansion on track.

All of the theme parks, in fact, are subject to constant renewal and expansion.

"The audience changes," says Tony Baxter, "and we have to change with it. That doesn't mean that everything has to be replaced. The Jungle Cruise has stayed the same for decades.

It's technologically crude, but it still works. But other things must change because the la thing we want is for any of the parks to be li a museum. . . . Even the pace of the rides ha change. When we put together a version of a Small World for Europe . . . we cut the rid from eleven minutes to eight minutes, and the interesting thing is that it seems right at that length. . . . People expect information to be delivered more quickly these days. That's why commercials run ten seconds now instead of ninety seconds."

The recent success of special-effects movies has certainly been an influence upon the way Imagineers think about any given ride. These movies are planned like amusement rides and the rides in turn reflect the technology of these films. The George Lucas Star Tours show, for example, derives directly from the *Star Wars* films on which it is based. A long-time fan of Disneyland, Lucas has been active in planning entertainments for the parks. This is just one sign of the way in which the parks have been expanding their horizons. Disney characters remain at the center of the whole enterprise – especially in areas like Mickey's Toontown at Disneyland – but anything is now possible so long as it partakes of the spirit that Disney conjured up at Anaheim in 1955.

More than seventy years have passed since Mickey Mouse first captured the imagination of the world and brought the Disney name to public prominence. It is almost forty-five years since Walt Disney launched the idea of the theme park. And there has not been a point in those decades when the Disney organization has not been moving forward on some front, whether pioneering the animated feature film or building a theme park as radical as EPCOT Center, not to mention reinventing the Broadway musical.

There were times when Walt Disney literally had to mortgage his home in order to realize his next project. That has certainly changed, and perhaps the greatest achievement of Michael Eisner and the late Frank Wells has been to build an organization in which no project, however ambitious, need be aborted or placed on the back burner for lack of funding. To have done this while encouraging a level of creativity that has produced films like *Beauty and the Beast* and *Who Framed Roger Rabbit*, and theme parks like Disney-MGM Studios and Disney's Animal Kingdom, makes that achievement all the more remarkable.

A question often asked in Disney circles is "What is the Disney secret?" The answer is "The persistence of the Disney legacy." It was established by Walt Disney himself, built upon by his handpicked team of artists, and now it has been taken up by another generation that understands that the legacy involves both respect for tradition and the willingness to take risks in the quest for new achievements.

The Disney legacy represents more than seven decades of accumulated knowledge – a legacy that is unique in the history of popular culture.

Imagineering concept art from 20,000 Leagues Under the Sea, an attraction at Disney's latest theme park, Tokyo Disney Seas, scheduled to open in the fall of 2001 on a site adjacent to Tokyo Disneyland Park

Index

Page numbers in *italics* refer to
illustrations

A

ABC (American Broadcasting
    Company), 126, 127, 128, 137
    Paramount Theaters group, 139
The Absent-Minded Professor, 129
Academy Awards, 12, 59, 98, 102, 127
*The Adventures of Ichabod and
    Mr. Toad*, 78
Aircraft Carrier Landing Signals, 76
Aladdin, 104, 105, 105–7
Alexander, Lloyd, 89
Algar, Jim, 55
Alice Comedies, 18, 126
Alice in Wonderland, 81–82, 82
Alice's Wonderland, 15–17, 17, 18
Allers, Roger, 107
Alwaleed, Prince of Saudi Arabia, 156
Andersen, Hans Christian, 98
Andrews, Julie, 130, 130
Animated feature films, 48–75, 157
Animation drawings, 51, 53, 59, 84, 85,
    98, 144, 145
    computer-generated 3-D, 95, 97, 98,
        108, 119, 120, 121, 122, 124
    effects, 68, 68, 98, 107, 112
    stop-action, 135, 136
"Anthology" film, 76. *See also* "Package"
    film
Aquino, Ruben, 90
The Aristocats, 86, 87
Armageddon, 137
Ashman, Howard, 97–98, 100, 103, 105,
    115–17
Audio-Animatronics, 144, 144–45, 145
Azadani, Rasoul, 105

B

Babbitt, Art, 31, 38, 40, 40–41, 53, 62, 70, 95
Babes in the Woods, 28
Bach, Johann Sebastian, 68
Bacher, Hans, 110
Background painting, 42, 43, 56, 62, 65,
    74, 75, 79, 81, 83, 84, 86, 97, 98, 99, 115
Bambi, 74, 75, 75
The Band Concert, 35
Barrie, Sir James, 82, 82
Basil of Baker Street, 90, 91. *See also The
    Great Mouse Detective*
Baskett, James, 126, 137

Baxter, Tony, 153–55, 156
Beatty, Warren, 132, 134
Beauty and the Beast, 100–102, 101, 102,
    103, 105
Bedknobs and Broomsticks, 131
Beethoven, Ludwig von, 68, 69, 70–71, 124
The Black Cauldron, 89, 90–91, 91
Blackton, J. Stuart, 12
Blue Rhythm, 25
Boat Builders, 43
Brandstater, Justin, 113
Bray, J.R., 14
Brizzi, Paul and Gaëtan, 125
Broken Toys, 53
A Bug's Life, 119, 122, 123
Burton, Tim, 90, 135
Butcher, Harold, 36
Butoy, Hendel, 124, 125

C

California Institute of the Arts, 90
Cannon, Johnny, 26
CAPS system, 98–99, 100
Caricatures, 41, 53
Carroll, Lewis, 81–82, 82
Carroll, Pat, 98
"Cels," 14, 99
The Chain Gang, 27
Chaplin, Charlie, 12, 36
Character development, 20–21, 31–33,
    48–51, 55–57, 61, 82, 83
Chicago, 10, 12
    McKinley High School, 12
    Symphony Orchestra, 124
    Tripp Avenue, 11
Chouinard Art School, Los Angeles, 40
Churchill, Frank, 28, 30, 58
Cinderella, 80, 81, 81, 82
CinemaScope format, 81, 82, 83
Clair, René, 36
Clark, Les, 21, 26
Clements, Ron, 87, 88, 97, 98, 105, 115
Cock of the Walk, 41
Codrick, Tom, 42, 75
The Color of Money, 132
Columbia Pictures, 27
"Concept art," 28, 49, 50, 69, 97, 102, 104,
    110, 113, 120
"The Concert Feature," 67. *See also
    Fantasia*
Continuity script or drawings, 22, 44
Cutting, Jack, 39

D

DaGradi, Don, 130
Daisy Duck, 125
Davis, Marc, 40, 83, 85
Davis, Virginia, 15, 18
Davy Crockett, 127–28, 128
Dead Poet's Society, 132, 133
Deja, Andreas, 90, 102, 105, 109
Dempster, Al, 86
Der Fuehrer's Face, 76
De Trémaudan, Frenchy, 40
Dickens, Charles, 95
Dick Tracy, 132, 134
Dippy Dawg, 31. *See also* Goofy
Disney, Diane (daughter), 47
Disney, Edna Francis (sister-in-law),
    17, 19
Disney, Elias (father), 10–12, 11
Disney, Flora Call (mother), 10, 11
Disney, Herbert (brother), 10
Disney, Lillian Bounds (wife), 17–18, 19,
    20, 47
Disney, Raymond (brother), 10
Disney, Roy E. (nephew), 90–91, 98, 99,
    119, 124, 131
Disney, Roy O. (brother), 10, 12, 15, 16, 17,
    18, 19, 23, 26–27, 47, 126, 138, 141, 142
Disney, Ruth (sister), 10, 19
Disney, Sharon (daughter), 47
Disney, Walter Elias, 16, 26, 40, 60
    and Alice Comedies, 18
    behind the camera, 14
    birthplace of, 11
    with Buddy Ebsen, 144
    death of, 86, 141
    as director, 17
    at Disneyland, 139
    early cartoons of, 12
    early enterprises of, 10–19, 82
    innovations by, 76–89, 126–27
    in Kansas City Film Ad Service, 13
    in Laugh-O-Grams office, 15
    with Laurel and Hardy, 37
    legacy of, 157
    marriage of, 17–18, 19, 20, 47
    receiving Academy Award, 59
    at Riviera Polo Grounds, 47
    success of, 36–39, 142–44
    voice of, 24
    with Walt Pfeiffer, 11
Disney Art School, Los Angeles, 41

The Disney Channel, 137
The Disney Institute, 151
Disneyland, 83, 127, 137, 138–40
    imaginary aerial view of, 140
    Main Street, 139, 139
    Mickey's Toontown, 143, 157
    Town Square, 140, 142
Disneyland Paris, 142, 153–56, 154
    The Château, 155
Disneyland series, 127–28
Donald Duck, 30–31, 32, 35, 45, 67, 76,
    78, 79, 125
Donald's Cousin Gus, 45
Donald's Golf Game, 45
Donald's Nephews, 45
Dreamland, 152
Duck Tales: The Movie, 119
Dukas, Paul, 67, 68, 70
Dumbo, 71–73, 72, 73

E

Earle, Eyvind, 83
Ebsen, Buddy, 128, 144
Edouarde, Carl, 23
Ed Wood, 135
Eisner, Michael, 90–91, 91, 126, 131, 148,
    149, 151, 153, 157
Elgar, Sir Edward, 125
Emerson, John, 112
EPCOT Center, 141, 142, 146–49, 151
    Disney-MGM Studios, 100, 117,
    149–50, 150, 151
        Indiana Jones Adventure, 150, 151
        Tower of Terror, 150, 150
    Horizons exhibit, 149
    Spaceship Earth, 147
    World Showcase, 148, 148, 149
EuroDisney, 153. *See also* Disneyland Paris
Experimental Prototype Community of
    Tomorrow. *See* EPCOT Center

F

Fantasia, 67–71, 68, 69, 70, 71, 75
Fantasia 2000, 119, 124, 125
Father of the Bride, 135
"Feature Symphony," 48
Felix the Cat, 143
Ferguson, Norm, 31, 34, 40, 55, 61–62
Fire Chief, 44
Fleischer, Max, 14, 48
Flowers and Trees, 28, 29

Food Will Win the War, 76
Foster, Harve, 126
The Fox and the Hound, 87–88, *89*
The Fox Hunt, 45
Freaky Friday, 131
Fun and Fancy Free, 78
Funicello, Annette, 128, *129*

G

Gabriel, Mike, 113
Gallopin' Gaucho, 21, 24, *24*
Gaskill, Andy, 87
Gay, Margie, 16, 17, *17*
George Lucas Star Tours, 156–57
Geronimi, Clyde, *40*
Gillett, Bert, 26
Gillmore, Jean, *106*
Glebas, Francis, 125
The Goddess of Spring, 32, 53
Goethe, Johann Wolfgang von, 67
Goetz, Dave, 114
Gogol, Darek, 114
Goldberg, Eric, 105, 107, 113, *125*
Good Morning, Vietnam, 132
Goofy, 31, *38*, 46, 76, *77*, 78
Goofy and Wilbur, 46
A Goofy Movie, 119
Gossett, Leroy, 12
Graham, Don, 40–41, 53
Grahame, Kenneth, 78
Grant, Joe, 51, 67
The Great Mouse Detective, 91–92, *92*
Grieg, Edvard, 26
Gulliver Mickey, 35

H

Hahn, Don, 88, 100, 107
Hamilton, Ham, 16
Hammerstein, Oscar, II, 58–59
Hardy, Oliver, *37*, *41*
Harline, Leigh, *40*, 58, 63
Harman, Hugh, 15, *16*, 18
Harman, Walker, 15, *16*
Hench, John, 141, 142–44
Hennesy, Hugh, *40*, 42
Henson, Jim, 150
Hercules, 115, *115*–17
Hollywood Pictures, 131, 135
Home Improvement, 137
Honey, I Blew Up the Kid, 132
Honey, I Shrunk the Kids, 132, 135
Hopkins, Paul, *40*
Howard, Ron, 131
Huemer, Dick, *40*, *40*, 67
Hugo, Victor, 114, *114*
The Hunchback of Notre Dame, *114*, 114–15
Hunt, Pixote, 124
Hurd, Earl, 14
Hurter, Albert, 28, *28*, *40*, 50, 51, 62

I

Imagineers, 138, 141, 142, 144, 145, 146, *147*, 148, 149, 155, 156
"Inspiration drawings," 28, *28*, 62. *See also* "Concept art"
Irving, Washington, 78
Ising, Rudolf "Rudy," 15, *16*, 18
Iwerks, Ubbe "Ub," *13*, 15, *16*, 17, 18, 20, *21*, 26, *26*–27, *27*, 85

J

Jackson, Wilfred, 21, *25*, 26, *40*
Jenkins, Chris, *112*
Jobs, Steve, 119
John, Elton, 109
Johnston, Ollie, 75, 86, 88, 95
José Carioca, 76, *77*
The Jungle Book, 85–86, *86*

K

Kahl, Milt, 55, 75, 86, 95
Kamen, Kay, 36
Kansas City Art Institute, 10
Kansas City Film Ad Service, 13, 14, 15
Kansas City Slide Company, 12
The Karnival Kid, 24
Katzenberg, Jeffrey, 91, 97, 109
Keane, Glen, 87, 88, *101*, *102*, *112*, 113–14, *118*
Keene, Lisa, *114*
Keisi Electric Railway Company, 152
Kelly, Walt, *41*
Kimball, Ward, *41*, 71, *73*
King, Jack, 26
King Neptune, 28
Kipling, Rudyard, 85, *86*

L

Lady and the Tramp, 82, *83*
Larson, Eric, 55, 75
Lasseter, John, 90, 119, *131*
Laugh-O-Grams, 14, *14*–15
Laurel, Stan, *37*, *41*
Lawrence, Gay, *117*
Layout drawings, *32*, *42*, *43*, *62*, *65*, *82*, *117*
"Leica reel," 40
Levine, James, *124*
The Lion King, *106*, 107, *107*–9, *108*, *109*, *110*
The Little Mermaid, *96*, 97, *97*–98
Live-action/animation hybrid films, 15, 78, 92–95, *93*, 127, *130*
Live-action films, *83*, *92*, 126–37, 143–44
Lounsbery, John, 61–62, 86
The Love Bug, 131
Lucas, George, 119, 150, 156
Lullaby Land, 32
Lundy, Dick, *37*
Luske, Ham, 55
Lyon, Red, 15

M

Make Mine Music, 78
The Many Adventures of Winnie the Pooh, 86
Mary Poppins, 130, *130*
Mattinson, Burny, 88
Maxwell, Carmen "Max," 15
McCay, Winsor, 13
Melody Time, 78
Melville, Herman, 149
Menken, Alan, 97, 98, 100, 105, 115–17
MGM/UA, 149–50
Mickey Cuts Up, 27
Mickey Mouse, 20–33, *22*, *23*, 36, *37*, 66, 67, 70, 78, *143*
  advertising for, *33*
  model sheets for, *25*, 43–47
  in Toontown, *143*
The Mickey Mouse Club, 128, *129*
Mickey's Amateurs, 46
Mickey's Circus, 38
Mickey's Fire Brigade, 42
Mickey's Garden, 43
Mickey's Surprise Party, 34
Midnight in a Toy Shop, 119
The Mighty Ducks, 135
Miki Kuchi, 27. *See also* Mickey Mouse
Miller, Ron (son-in-law), 89, 131
Milne, A.A., 86, 88
Milotte, Al and Elma, 127
Minkoff, Rob, 107
Minnie Mouse, *23*, 24, 27, 34
"Minnie's Yoo Hoo," 26
Mintz, Charles, 17–18, 20
Miramax films, 131
Model sheets, *25*, 43–47, 51, *106*
Moore, Fred, *38*, *41*, 43–47, 53, 57, *57*, 62
Moose Hunters, 39
Morris the Midget Moose, 81
Mortimer, 20. *See also* Mickey Mouse
Mother Goose Goes Hollywood, 41
Mouseketeers, *129*
Moving Day, 38
Mulan, 116, 117, *117*, 150
Musker, John, 88, 91, 97–98, 105, 115
Mussorgsky, Modest, 68, 71, *71*

N

Nash, Clarence "Ducky," 30–31
National Biscuit Company, 34
National Hockey League franchise, 135
Naturalism, 14, *64*, 74, 75, 92
Natwick, Grim, 55, 95
New York World's Fair (1964), 141, 147
  "Great Moments with Mr. Lincoln," 144–45, *145*
The Nightmare Before Christmas, 135, *136*

O

O'Day, Dawn, 17
Oliver & Company, 95, *95*, 95–97
One Hundred and One Dalmatians, 84, *85*, *85*
Orphan's Benefit, 31, 35
Oswald the Lucky Rabbit, 17–18, *19*, 20, 24

P

"Package" film, 76–78, *77*, 126
Paramount Theaters group. *See* ABC
The Parent Trap, 129
Pegleg Pete, 27
"Pencil test," 40
Pentecost, James, 114
People and Places series, 127
"Persistence of vision" theory, 13
Peter Pan, 82, *82*
Pfeiffer, Walt, 10–12, *11*
Phillippi, Charles, *42*
Photography
  multiplane, 51–53, 83, 99
  stop-action, 14
  underwater, 64
  Xerox, *84*, 85
Pickford, Mary, 37
Pierné, Gabriel, 70
Pinocchio, 60, *61*, 61–63, *62*, *63*, *64*, 65, 71
Pioneer Days, 28
Pixar animation company, 119, *120*, *122*, *123*
Plane Crazy, 21, 24
Plateau, Joseph Antoine, 13
Plateau-Stampfer device, 13
Playful Pluto, 31, 34
Pluto, 27, 31, *38*, 76
Pluto's Dream House, 47
Pocahontas, *112*, *113*, 113–14
Polar Trappers, 43
Pollyanna, 129
Ponchielli, Amilcare, 68, *70*, 71
Powers, Pat, 23–24, 26–27
Pretty Woman, 132, *133*
Puss in Boots, 14

R

Reitherman, Wolfgang "Woolie," 62, 87–88
The Reluctant Dragon, 126
"Repertoire program," *124*
The Rescuers, 87, *89*, 98
The Rescuers Down Under, 98–99, *99*
Respighi, Ottorino, 125
Rice, Tim, 105, 109
Riviera Polo Grounds, 47, *47*
Roberts, Bill, *40*
Robin Hood, 87
Rob Roy, the Highland Rogue, 126–27
Rodgers, Richard, 58–59

159

Roget, Peter Mark, 13
Rotoscoping, 59
Ruthless People, 132
Ryman, Herb, *140*

S

Saint-Saëns, Camille, *125*
Sai Ping Lok, *117*
Salten, Felix, 75
Saludos Amigos, 76, *77*
Schneider, Peter, 92, 97, 98
Schubert, Franz, 68, 71, *71*
Schumacher, Tom, 107
Scott, Retta, 75
Seal Island, 127
Sears, Ted, 43
The Shaggy Dog, 129
Sharp, Margery, 87, *89,* 98
Sharpsteen, Ben, 26
Sherman, Richard M. and Robert B., 130
Shostakovich, Dmitri, *124*
Silly Symphonies, 26, 28–30, *41,* 48, 53, 81
Sister Act, 135
The Skeleton Dance, 26, *27*
Sklar, Marty, 142, 147, 151
Sleeping Beauty, 83, *83*
Slide Donald Slide, 79
Smith, Paul, 58
Smith, Sidney, 14
Smith, Webb, 27, *34*
Snow White and the Seven Dwarfs, 41,
    48–59, *49, 50, 51, 52, 53, 54, 55, 56, 57,*
    58, 59, 63
So Dear to My Heart, 126
Song of the South, 78, *78,* 126, *127*
Son of Flubber, 129
The Sorcerer's Apprentice, 66, 67. See also
    Fantasia
Sound tracks, 21–23, *23,* 24, 26, 58–59,
    62–63, 98
Spacey, Kevin, 119
Spielberg, Steven, 92
Splash!, 131, *132*
Stalling, Carl, 26, *26, 27, 27*
Stampfer, Simon Ritter von, 13
Steamboat Willie, 22, 23, 23–24
Stevenson, Robert Louis, 127
Stokowski, Leopold, 67–68
Storyboards, 27–28, *52,* 63, 64, 66, 95, 144.
    See also "Leica reel"
Story conferences, 27, 55–58, *60,* 92
The Story of Robin Hood and his Merrie
    Men, 126–27
Stravinsky, Igor, 68, *68,* 70, *125*
Susie the Little Blue Coupe, 81
Swiss Family Robinson, 129
The Sword and the Rose, 126–27
The Sword in the Stone, 85
Symbolist movement, 69

T

Tarzan, 118, 119
Taylor, Deems, 67
Taymor, Julie, 109, *111*
Tchaikovsky, Peter Ilich, *68,* 68–70
Technicolor process, 28, *29*
Technirama format, 83
Television, 127–28, *128,* 137
Temple, Shirley, 59
Tenggren, Gustav, *61, 62*
Theme parks, 138–45
Thomas, Frank, 53, 59, 75, 86, 88, 95
The Three Caballeros, 76
3-D animation, *120. See also* Animation
    drawings
Three Little Pigs, 28–30, *30, 31*
Three-strip system, 28. *See also*
    Technicolor process
Thru the Mirror, 42
Tin Men, 132
Tokyo Disneyland Park, 142, 152–53, *157*
Tokyo Disney Seas, *157*
"Toons," 92, *94*
Toot, Whistle, Plunk and Boom, 81
Topolino, 27. *See also* Mickey Mouse
Touchstone films, 131, 132
Towns, Donald, *97*
Toy Story, 119, *120,* 121
Toy Story II, 121
Tracy, Spencer, 47, *47*
Travers, P.L., 130
Treasure Island, 126–27, *128*
Tron, 131, *131*
Trousdale, Gary, 100, 114
True-Life Adventures series, 127
20,000 Leagues Under the Sea, 128–29,
    129, 157
Tytla, Vladimir "Bill," 53, 61, 71, 88, 95

U

Uncle Remus stories, 78, *78,* 126, *127*
Universal Pictures, 17–18

V

Vander Wende, Richard, *104, 105*
Ventura, Valerio, *117*
Verne, Jules, 128, 155
Victory Through Air Power, 76
Victory Vehicles, 76, *77*
Voice talent, 24, 50, 55, 86, 98, 119

W

Walker, Card, 148
Wallace, Ollie, 58
Walsh, Bill, 130, 131
The Walt Disney Company, 90–91, *91,*
    109, 126, 135, 137
Walt Disney Pictures, 91
Walt Disney Productions, 148
Walt Disney Studios, 86–89, 90–91, 98
    in Burbank, 63, 75, 91, 113, *130, 135,* 138
    in Glendale, 91, 100
    at Hyperion Avenue, 17–33, *33,* 40, 41,
        59, 63
    unionization at, 73
Walt Disney World, 141–45, 146, 151
    Big Thunder Mountain, *143*
    Celebration town, 151, *153*
    Cinderella Castle, *142*
    Disney's Animal Kingdom, 151, *152*
    Haunted Mansion, *85*
    The Magic Kingdom, *141,* 146, 149, *155*
    Tomorrowland, *156*
Warner Brothers, 92
Washington, Ned, 63
WDI (Walt Disney Imagineering), 138,
    141, 142
Weber, Kem, 63
WED (Walter Elias Disney), 138, 142
Weis, Bob, 150
Wells, Frank, 90, 109, 131, 149, 157
Wells, H.G., 36
Western Printing and Lithographing, 139
White, T.H., 85
Who Framed Roger Rabbit, 92–95, *93,*
    94, 98
Who Killed Cock Robin?, 53
Wilder, Thornton, 36
Wilhite, Tom, 131
Williams, Richard, *93,* 95
Williams, Robin, 107, 132, *133*
Williams, Rowland B., *97*
Winkler, Margaret J., 15, 17
Winnie the Pooh and the Blustery Day,
    86, *88*
Winnie the Pooh and the Honey Tree, 86
Winnie the Pooh and Tigger Too, 86
Winter, 28
Wise, Kirk, 100, 114
The Wise Little Hen, 30–31, *32*
Wolf, Gary K., 92
Wong, Tyrus, 75
Woolverton, Linda, 100

Z

Zemeckis, Robert, *93,* 95
Zippel, David, *117*
Zoetrope, 13